MW01125815

Telling Fortunes

By Tea Leaves

How to Read Your Fate in a Teacup

By Cicely Kent

With Twenty Illustrations

Revised and Updated, 2020

Edited by Anthony Whitman,
Ryan Starling

Printed in the United States of America

Cover by Jessica Tiderman

ISBN-13: 978-0-9960638-5-2

Sage & Hawthorn Print, LLP
www.sagehawthorn.com

CONTENTS

I. Introduction to the Divination by Tea-Leaves

At no time in the history of the world has there been such earnest searching for light and knowledge in all matters relating to Psychic Phenomena as in the present day. The desire to investigate some new disclosure has resulted in yet other discoveries. Such will be handed on in their various forms to be studied and used by those who seek to learn.

Few subjects need more patience than those dealing with Psychology. Even those who put their knowledge to a practical use in such studies as divination by tea-leaves, must still plod patiently along a path thickly strewn with new knowledge. The powers of clairvoyance, for instance, cannot be forced or hurried; such arbitrary laws as time have no meaning for the subconscious self, therefore the need for hurry does not exist.

I was once told by a very mediumistic woman that she had sat in the same room at the same time for an hour every day for seven years, because she "wished to develop Clairvoyance." Here was patience indeed! In some manifestations of the clairvoyant powers within us, it is spontaneous, the closing of the eyes to shut out all material surroundings being all that is necessary to bring a vision of what is happening, or shortly to happen, possibly hundreds of miles away.

In all dreams the clairvoyant powers are spontaneous; but for the development of clairvoyance at will, great perseverance is necessary. Its interests and powers are unlimited, so that it is well worth the patience and time spent upon it.

In the use of tea-leaves as a means of divination, the more developed the "clear sight," the more interesting and accurate will be the interpretation. Practice is most necessary, especially for those who have less natural clairvoyance than others.

The desire for knowledge on all Psychic matters has led to an increased demand for various methods of bringing into symbols and pictures that hidden knowledge of the present and the future. That this knowledge can be translated to us symbolically is apparent to everyone—who could doubt it, and still believe in anything at all?

Tea-leaves are habitually used by many people as a means of divination.

1

To some it is an easier method than the cards, as there is less to memorise, or the crystal.

There is in Paris a famous clairvoyant who always uses tea-leaves as the medium for her powers of divination. Some are inclined to jeer at the fortune in the teacup, but if the language of symbolism is rightly understood, the medium through which it is seen matters little.

Tea-leaves have the advantage of being simple, inexpensive, and within the reach of everyone. It cannot be claimed that the cult is of the greatest antiquity; for although it seems to have been used in China from very early times, tea was not brought into Europe until about the middle of the sixteenth century. For many years after its introduction into this country, tea was far too costly to be used except by a comparatively small proportion of the population. It has, however, proved its extreme usefulness as a means of divination, as well as its merits as a beverage, for close upon three centuries.

It is a very favourite method with the Highlanders, where it is customary for the "guid wife" to read in her cup of tea at breakfast the events she may look for during the day. Simple though they may probably be, there are to be seen in the tea-leaves, a letter, a parcel, a visitor, a wedding, and so on. It is said that no Highland seer would take money for making prognostications as to the future. This, no doubt, is one good reason for their powers as clairvoyants.

It is a misfortune that clairvoyance should ever have to come into the material necessities of money transactions, as it tends to mar the clear vision.

It is said by some that tea-leaves can foretell the events for twenty-four hours only. As clairvoyance has no restrictions as to time or space, I cannot see how it can be thus laid down as a fact that it is limited to man-made laws of time! Certainly there is much evidence of the "tea leaves" being capable of foreseeing events of an important nature at a considerable distance ahead.

One of the most difficult points in interpreting visions of clairvoyance is the time element; simply because time, as we know it, does not exist. The intuitive faculty is needed for any accurate definition of time, so important to us in our present conditions, so absolutely unimportant to the subconscious self. Let us decide at once, then, that divination by tea-leaves may, and often does, extend to a further vision than that of the twenty-four hours. Much depends upon the methods used.

Our individual past, quite apart from the arbitrary laws of heredity, makes the road of our future. Possibly this may account for the curious fact that in dreams the setting is often in childhood's surroundings, while the dream itself is obviously of the present or the future. This shows how the first beginnings of the event which is to come were brought about. It is somewhat like unwinding a cotton reel!

There are, no doubt, some who look upon the tea-leaves merely as a form of amusement, and who entertain their friends in that way. Well, it is a harmless amusement, and is often useful at a very dull tea party! But for those who take it seriously, and regard it as one of the many means of divination, it will be treated with the respect due to such matters.

As in other forms of divination, so with the reading of the tea-cup, a great deal depends on the seer. Those who are naturally clairvoyant will read many events and scenes in the cup which would be passed over by others not so gifted. Even without this "clear sight," however, the tea-leaves may be read by anyone who has learned the principles and the symbolic meanings given in this book. With a certain amount of intuition and imagination, the tea-cups may be most successfully used to reveal the future.

II. Practice and Method

A wide, shallow cup is the best kind to use for tea-leaf divination—white if possible. A narrow cup adds to the seer's difficulties, as the tea-leaves cannot be plainly seen. Small cups, too, are objectionable for the same reason, and a fluted cup is even worse. A plain, even surface is required, with no pattern of any kind, as this has a tendency to confuse the symbols. Lower quality and the cheaper mixtures, which contain so much dust and twigs are of no use for reading a fortune, as they cannot form into pictures and symbols that can easily be distinguished.

Those who desire to have their tea-leaves interpreted should leave about a teaspoonful of tea at the bottom of the cup. It should then be taken in the left hand, and turned three times from left with a quick swing. Then very gently, slowly, and with care, turn it upside down over the saucer, leaving it there for a minute, so that all the moisture may drain away.

Some diviners of the tea-leaves insist on a concentration of the mind during this turning of the cup, as do many cartomancers whilst the cards are being shuffled; others prefer the mind to be as far as possible free from any definite thought or desire, simply allowing it to dwell on such abstract subjects as flowers or the weather. Personally, I advocate this for both systems of divination; it enables the subconscious mind to assert itself unhindered, whilst the normal mind is in abeyance.

The turning of the cup before inverting it over the saucer is equivalent to the shuffling of the cards. It is as a direct result of those few seconds turning that the pictures and signs are created, the subconscious mind directing the hand holding the cup. The following simple ritual is all that is necessary to those consulting the tea-leaves.

The cup to be read is held by the seer and turned about as necessary, so that the symbols may be read without disturbing them. This is important, but no disturbance will take place if the moisture has been properly drained away. The handle of the cup represents the consultant, also the home, or, if the consultant be away from home the present abode.

It is necessary to have a starting point in the cup for the purpose of indicating events approaching near to, or far distant from, the person consulting. The leaves near the rim denote such things as may be expected to occur quickly; those directly beneath the handle indicate present and

4

immediate happenings; those on the sides of the cup suggest more distant events; whilst those at the bottom deal with the far distant future.

This method of fixing the time, coupled with intuition, renders it possible to give a consultant some idea as to when an event may be expected; but if there be no intuitive sense of time, it will be found wiser not to be too positive.

The turning of the cup and the draining of the moisture having been carried out as directed, the tea-leaves will be found distributed at the sides and bottom of the cup.

For those who wish to use the saucer as a further means of divination, the following suggestions will be useful.

There must be a definite point to represent the consultant, and for this reason the saucer is usually rejected. There is also the objection that it is more difficult to manipulate in the turning. Nevertheless, it is found to give excellent results, and, if the cup is bare of events, it is useful to be able to find information in the saucer.

First of all, then, to determine the position of the consultant. Take the centre of the saucer for this purpose. The circle round it represents the home, or if the consultant is away from home, the present abode, and also events near at hand. The more distant circle indicates those things which are not to be expected for some time. The outer circle and rim suggest events as yet in the misty future.

When the saucer is used as an additional means of seeking knowledge of coming events, after the symbols in the cup have been exhausted, it will often be found that this secondary divination confirms or enlarges upon that which has already been foretold in the cup.

The moisture and leaves drained from the cup, having remained in the saucer, should be turned by the consultant three times with the same swirling motion as for the cup, and the moisture carefully poured away. The saucer should be held inverted for a few seconds, otherwise when it is placed upright, the remaining moisture will disturb the tea-leaves. The symbols are read in exactly the same way as in the cup, the only difference being the positions representing the consultant, the home, and the indications of time. These have already been explained.

5

III. General Theories in Reading the Cup

At first sight the interior of the cup will show the leaves scattered about apparently haphazard and with no arrangement; just a jumble of tea-leaves and nothing more. In reality they have come to their positions and have taken on the shapes of the symbols for which they stand, by the guidance of the subconscious mind directing the hand in the turning of the cup.

The various shapes and the meanings to be attached to them will at first be puzzling to beginners. A good deal of practice is necessary before the tea-leaf symbols can be accurately interpreted at a glance. That, however, will come later, and in time it will be as easy as reading a book.

If you wish to be a proficient reader of the tea-leaves, practise constantly this interpretation of the shapes and positions of the leaves. Take a cup and follow out the simple instructions for the turning and draining of it, and then carefully study the result.

It is an excellent plan to make a rough copy of the leaves as they present themselves to you in each cup, making notes of the various meanings.

Do not feel dismayed if, when you begin looking at the tea-leaves, you are unable to discover in them anything definitely symbolic. It is certain that nothing will be found if the seer is feeling nervous! Keep a calm, open mind, and do not be in a hurry, for it is under such conditions only that a clear reading of the leaves will be possible. In some cases the symbols are more easily read than in others. Much depends upon the consultant.

The gift of imagination (by no means to be confused with invention) is of the greatest possible importance in discerning the symbols which are of such endless shapes and variety. The seer has to find in the forms of the tea-leaves a resemblance, sometimes it may be but a faint one, to natural objects, e.g., trees, houses, flowers, bridges, and so forth. Figures of human beings and animals will frequently be seen, as will squares, triangles, circles, and also the line of fate.

These signs may be large or small, and the importance of them must be judged by their relative size and position. Suppose, for instance, that a small cross should be at the bottom of the cup, the only one to be seen, the seer would predict that a trifling vexation or a tiresome little delay must be expected; but not for the present, as it is at the bottom of the cup. An alphabetical list of symbols is given later on, so it is not necessary to define them here. The various points of a more general character, however, must be studied before it is possible to give an accurate reading.

It will constantly be found that the stems, isolated leaves, or small groups of leaves, form a letter of the alphabet, sometimes a number. These letters and numbers have meanings which must be looked for in connection with other noticeable signs. If an initial "M" appears, and near to it a small square or oblong leaf, both being near the rim of the cup, it would indicate a letter coming speedily from someone whose name begins with an "M". If the initial appears near the bottom of the cup it shows that the letter will not be coming for some time.

If there be a clear space at the bottom of the cup devoid of tea-leaves, it shows water, and that, in all probability, the letter is coming from abroad. If the symbol of the letter comes very near to a bird flying, it shows a telegram. If the bird is flying towards the consultant (the handle), the telegram has been received. The news in it is to be judged by other signs in the cup. If flying away from the handle, the telegram is sent by the consultant. A single bird flying always indicates speedy news.

In a cup with various ominous signs, such as a serpent, an owl, or many crosses, the news coming is not likely to be pleasant. In a cup without bad signs, it can safely be said that the news is good.

As a general rule large letters indicate places, whilst smaller ones give the names of persons. Thus a large letter "E" would stand for Edinburgh and a smaller "E" for Edwards, for instance. To all rules there comes the occasional exception, and this principle holds good with regard to the letters in the tea-cup. It is said that these smaller letters always point to the first letter of the surname. Usually it is so; but I have constantly found from experience that it is the first letter of the birth (Christian) name, or even a pet name, to which the letter refers. It is well to keep this possibility in mind, otherwise the seer may give misleading information to consultants.

Sometimes numbers mean the date for an event to be expected, a "5" for instance, very near the brim of the cup, or the handle (the consultant), means in five days; or five weeks if it come on the side, possibly as far off as five months if the figure be at the bottom of the cup.

As dots around a symbol always indicate money in some form or another, according to the character of the symbol, a figure beside the dots would signify the amount of money to be expected. If the symbol were that of a legacy with the figure "90" near, it would show that a little legacy of ninety pounds might be anticipated.

Clearly defined symbols that stand out separately are of more importance than such as are difficult to discern. Clusters of shapeless leaves represent clouds marring the effect of an otherwise fortunate cup.

Journeys are shown by lines or dots formed by the dust and smaller leaves of the tea. The length and direction of the journey may be known by the extent of the line and, roughly speaking, the point of the compass to which it leads, the handle in this case representing south. If the line of dots ascends sharply to the brim of the cup, a journey to a hilly country will be taken.

Supposing the consultant to be at home, and the dots form a line from the handle all round the cup and back to the handle, it signifies a journey for a visit and the return. If the line were to stop before reaching the handle again, with an appearance of a house where the line ends, a change of residence might safely be predicted. A wavy line shows indecision as to arrangements. Crosses upon the line indicate that there will be vexation or delay in connection with the journey. Large flat leaves some distance apart along the line stand for important stations to be passed through.

For some consultants there seems very little of interest to be read in their cup. There are no events, merely trivialities. It is therefore difficult to find anything that could be considered as "future", when it seems to be just a dead level "present", the daily life, nothing more. It is sad for those who have such a dull life, but there is usually some sign, a small happening such as a parcel, or a visit from a friend. These must be made the most of. The pleasure of anticipation will add to the realisation.

A confused looking tea-cup, without any definite symbols, just a muddle of tea-leaves, is useless for the purpose of divination, beyond giving an indication of the state of the consultant's mind, so vague and undecided in its character that it obscures everything. Tell such a one the reason for the failure of divining, and recommend a more reliable state of mind. Then let them try their "fortune" again in a few months, when it may be found quite different.

It is of course a great mistake to be always "looking in the tea-leaves", as some foolish people do twice a day. It is sure to lead to contradictions though there is no harm in the habit of "looking in the cup" each morning as others do, for finding the events likely to happen in the course of the day. This is as permissible as the reading of the cards each morning for the day's events by those who consider it a safeguard, remembering that to be forewarned is to be forearmed.

Some people use the tea-cup simply for the purpose of asking a definite question, such as, "Is the sum of money I am expecting coming soon?" When this is the case, the consultant should be told before turning the cup in the hand to concentrate the thoughts on this one point, as in the case of wishing while shuffling the cards for a definite wish. Then the seer must look only for the signs that will give the answer to the question, ignoring all other points. This is necessary for the giving of a satisfactory answer to the question asked.

IV. Divination by Tea-Leaves as an Amusement

And as a More Serious Study

The need for patience cannot be too strongly impressed upon those who are beginning to learn the language of tea-leaves. Some of the most interesting symbols are very minute, and will certainly be missed by the seer who is in a hurry.

When tea-leaf reading is indulged in merely as an amusement to while away a few moments after a meal, a hasty glance at the cup, or cup and saucer, will suffice. The seer will just note the chief features, such as a journey, a letter, a parcel, or news of a wedding, and pass on to the next cup. But this is far from being a really interesting method of divination by tea-leaves, wherein so much knowledge is to be found, and so much useful information gained.

Those who closely study this fascinating subject will certainly be well rewarded by a deep personal interest, in addition to the pleasure they give to others.

It is wonderful how rapidly converts are made to this form of divination. Some who in the past have been heard scornfully to assert that they "have no belief in tea-leaves", become the most regular inquirers. Moreover, these sceptics have proved to be very efficient students.

There is always a satisfaction in persuading another to one's own point of view. The more obstinate the opposition, the more glorious the final conquest!

It is a rare occurrence nowadays to meet with three people in the course of a day, and not to find that one at least is deeply interested in fortune-telling in some of its various forms.

Quite recently, I had a letter from a girl who has gone on a visit to British Columbia, asking me if I would "do the cards" for her, as she could not find anyone in her vicinity who was particularly good at divination. She went on to say that, "there is a perfect rage for fortune-telling out here, and everyone is keen on it." Another instance of this universal popularity was given to me by a friend who had recently been to America. She was amazed at the numbers of women whom she saw absorbed in the reading of their tea-cups each day of the voyage.

The male sex holds aloof and leaves us to "perform these follies". Some ascribe it to man's superiority. Or as briefly summed up by a delightful member of their sex, who when declaiming against the possibility of the future being made visible, said, "With all apologies to you, I must say I am not so profoundly stupid as to believe in these things; it cannot be anything more than rot."

It is remarkable how such protests die away when clairvoyant evidence, either by cards, tea-leaves, or other means, has accurately predicted some event of the distant future that at the time appeared absurd and impossible of happening.

Woman may lawfully claim superiority with regard to her intuitive faculty, and thus she is well equipped for exercising her divining powers.

Who need be dull or bored when the language of symbolism remains to be learned? Perhaps I should say, studied; for completely learned it can never be, seeing that fresh events are constantly occurring in the world, and new symbols appear representing each.

There are few things more fascinating than personal discovery, and those who become students of divination by tea-leaves, or cards, may safely be promised a taste of this pleasing sensation of achievement. It is limited to the few to discover the marvels of radium, or the discomforts of the South Pole, but a fragment of their glory is shared by those who find new evidence of the far-reaching knowledge of symbolism.

V. Some Hints for Diviners

Remarkable Instances of Prophecy by the Tea-Leaves

"For a man's mind is sometimes wont to tell him more
than seven watchmen that sit above in a high tower."

To those of an inquiring or doubting turn of mind, there may arise the very natural question as to *why* one shaped tea-leaf should mean "a hat" and another "a table". It is useless to point out that these objects are perfectly represented by the leaves. That is of no practical satisfaction. The simple fact that each language has its alphabet, its spelling, and its words, which must be learned before there can be any reasonable understanding of it, seems the best and obvious reply.

Symbolism is a wide subject with many branches. Who can expect to master even its alphabet in a moment? To those who cannot accept the symbols in the tea-leaves on the authority of past experience, reaching over several centuries, I would recommend a careful study of their cups for, say, three months. Let them make notes of such signs as appear and beside them place their meanings and predictions.

At the end of this time, compare all that has taken place with these notes, and I think there will be no further lack of faith in the tea-leaf symbols.

Before very many years have passed the language of symbolism by cards, tea-leaves, crystal gazing, etc., will probably be almost universally understood. The day will undoubtedly come when it will be accepted as naturally as the English language, and we shall cease to worry ourselves as to the why and wherefore of it all.

It is important that those who are learning the art of divination by tea-leaves should realise the necessity for consistently attributing the same meanings to the symbols. Do not be tempted to change their interpretation for what may seem a more probable, or pleasant, prediction for your client. It is a fatal mistake.

Remember that you are dealing with conditions and events of the future which are outside the limited knowledge of the normal mind, whose power of vision is limited to physical sight.

A simple instance of what may occur, should you thus change the meanings of the symbols, will suffice to show the folly of such a practice.

A consultant comes to have her "fortune read". She is known to you personally, and you are aware that she is anxious to hear a hopeful report of someone dear to her who is ill. The tea-leaf symbols are obstinately unfavourable, and display ominous signs of forthcoming sorrow. If you gloss over this fact completely, and predict a rapid recovery from the illness, what becomes of your client's faith in the power of foretelling the future? Certain it is that the symbols would be right in their verdict, and you would be wrong.

It is usually easier to prophesy smooth things rather than unpleasant facts, but to do this in the face of obvious contradictions will lead to disaster in foretelling the future.

Divination by tea-leaves or cards has the candour to be frankly disagreeable when necessary. This is one great argument in favour of its unerring truthfulness. There is no means by which symbols may be coaxed into proclaiming false statements.

The most practised clairvoyant may occasionally make mistakes in her reading of the symbols, but no genuine seer should ever deliberately give a wrong interpretation of them to please her consultant. The business of the diviner is to give what she believes to be a correct and unprejudiced translation of the symbols before her.

It is sometimes a vexed question as to what extent information of a gloomy nature, which may appear in a divination, should be given to a client. Some are in favour of withholding such matter altogether, whilst others announce it frankly without modification. It seems impossible to lay down any hard and fast rule. There are so many things to be taken into account, and each case should be treated on its merits and according to its peculiar circumstances. There are some who would fret themselves ill at the least mention of coming misfortune, others would be the better prepared to meet it by having been warned of its approach.

One rule can be safely made for guidance on this point. Do not minimise danger when a timely warning may avert an accident, or other misfortune, nor should symbols of ill omen be exaggerated. As students become proficient, they will find many meanings in the tea-leaves in addition to those which they learn from this book. Much will depend upon circumstances and individual temperaments.

These personally discovered meanings should be carefully noted and verified with events as they occur.

It is necessary to remember that divination by the tea-cup is by no means limited to personal information. Forthcoming public events are frequently revealed. This adds largely to the interest and usefulness of the divination. It is important to point out this to consultants, so that they may not be too ready to fix the whole reading of their cups to purely personal matters. It will be found that public news is usually foretold in the cups of those who seek information of the future as a regular practice.

For those who rarely do so, private affairs alone will appear, probably without even a forecast of the weather to be expected within the next few days.

It is a curious fact that the wider knowledge should seem to be reserved for those who practise divination constantly, but so it is.

Some remarkable instances of the accurate foretelling of public events, which have quite recently been brought to my notice, may be interesting.

For some weeks before the coal strike of 1920 was declared, a pickaxe was seen on several occasions in the cups of two persons, both of whom read their tea-leaves regularly. This symbol, as will be seen in the dictionary which follows, stands for "labour trouble and strikes". A spade was also in evidence at intervals, a further sign of "trouble and unrest". It was through no fault of the tea-leaves if some of us were not in the superior position of knowing all about the strike before it came to pass.

The symbols already mentioned would of course apply equally to railway disturbance, and some time before the threat of a strike was announced, these symbols appeared again, together with an engine, and a signal at the angle of "Danger". This seemed ominous. But within a few days the signal was evident once more; but on this occasion set at "All Clear". So it was easy to decide that the threatened strike would not take place. The accuracy of this prediction by means of the tea-leaves was shortly afterwards made evident.

Again, a week before there seemed to be even a hope of a settlement of the coal strike, a mining shaft presented itself in one of the tea-cups which had previously been indicating the strike. This symbol appeared at the top of the cup standing out clearly by itself, evidently predicting the miners' return to work within a short time. There was no need to depend upon information from the newspapers as to the end of the strike, for here in the tea-leaves was all necessary evidence of the fact.

Another very remarkable instance of symbolism was given to me by a friend a short time ago. On Monday morning, October 26th, 1920, the three following symbols appeared in her cup:—

A vulture resting on a rock.

An eagle.

A monkey.

In the evening of that day the death of King Alexander of Greece was announced.

It will be seen, on referring to the dictionary, that an eagle and a vulture signify "the death of a monarch". The monkey who lay at the bottom of the cup, apparently dead, was of course the third symbol as having caused the King's death. It was particularly gratifying that these signs should have appeared in my friend's cup for she is a mathematical genius, and rejects every symbol which she cannot recognise at once. She was so struck by these signs that she called them to the attention of her mother, who also immediately perceived and identified them. The only regrettable omission was that the cup was not photographed. It would have been valuable evidence for the wonders of the tea-leaves.

This same friend had another interesting experience. The head of an Indian appeared in her cup, with other signs pointing to news of a personal nature. She was puzzled, for, as far as she knew, there was no one in India from whom she would be in the least likely to hear.

Very shortly afterwards, however, her mother went on a visit to London. There she quite unexpectedly met someone who had recently come from India, and who had brought back messages of remembrance and affection from a girl who my friend had no idea was in India at that time. Hence the Indian in her tea-cup!

Whilst on this subject, I am reminded of an occasion in another city, when criminals were represented in the tea-leaves. I was looking into my tea-cup one day, when I saw most clearly depicted two thieves creeping stealthily, their attitude making this evident. In their hands were what appeared to be knives, and they were making towards a figure that was unmistakably that of an officer. He was standing upon what looked like a raised platform with a barricade round him. He held a revolver in his hand.

I am quite aware that some may think this a tall tale for the tea-leaves to relate! But fortunately my reading of the cup was witnessed by two others, one of them being a man, who, although interested in psychic subjects, despises the tea-leaves! Without remarking upon what I saw, I suggested that he should look at my cup and see what he made of it. Without a moment's hesitation he said, "There is an officer defending himself against some natives who are about to attack him."

My readers will appreciate the satisfaction this testimony gave me, coming as it did from one who had never before looked into a cup. Moreover, that this witness should have been one of the male sex added to its value! This prediction of danger for someone in India was borne out by facts that were disclosed shortly afterwards. These instances which I have given illustrate the variety and interest which are to be found in divination by tea-leaves.

VI. Writing in the Tea-Leaves

Some Frequent Symbols

Another source through which messages are received by the tea-leaves will be found in the writing which will be seen from time to time. Moreover, it has the great advantage of being clear and easy to decipher, so that there may be no doubt of what is intended to be understood by it. The tea-leaves can never be accused of being illegible. Occasionally it is very minute writing, and would probably be passed over by those who read their cups in a superficial manner. To those who study them carefully the future is revealed.

No one would reasonably expect to find a speech from the Prime Minister or an invitation to a tea-party written for them in the tea-leaves. But words they certainly will find.

A short time ago I saw in my cup, in perfect copperplate writing, the word "wait". I was annoyed by it, for what is more annoying than having to wait? Sometimes it may happen that the tea-leaves—as with their relatives, the tumbler and automatic writing—become a little shaky in their spelling. But this is not a serious defect, and the trifling errors do not prevent the word from being translatable. It is a recognised fact that writing seen through a medium, whether it be tea-leaves, or a dream, is of importance, and should always be regarded with attention and with an endeavour to understand its message.

I should like to point out that certain figures and symbols are of so frequent occurrence that it may be well to emphasise their general significance by referring to them here, in addition to their meaning being given in the dictionary.

Among those which threaten misfortune, or sorrow, are the following: crosses, snakes, spades, pistols, guns, toads, cats.

Joy and success are indicated by such symbols as a crescent moon, clover leaves, flowers, trees, anchors, fruit, circles, stars.

Having learned the symbols and the combined symbols by heart, it will require only a little practice to interpret their meanings without hesitation. For those who find difficulty in committing the dictionary to memory, an essential for proficient reading of the cup, I would suggest that they write down any meaning which may seem especially hard to remember, roughly drawing its symbol beside it. In this way the difficulty will soon be overcome.

VII. The "Nelros" Cup

Two Example Readings of its Signs

"If thou wouldst learn thy future with thy tea,
This magic cup will show it thee."

Some readers may find an additional interest in divination by tea-leaves, if they use a cup marked with the planetary symbols, patented as the "Nelros Cup of Fortune". A short explanation of the symbols, and the method of using this cup, will be helpful for those who are not familiar with its signs. I am not suggesting the use of the "Nelros" saucer, for the reason that its signs are somewhat obscure, and students who have no experience in the science of astrology would find it confusing, if used in addition to the cup, in which all needful signs are illustrated.

As in the case of the ordinary tea-cup, the handle remains as the representative of the consultant. The turning of it and draining of the moisture should be carried out in the usual way.

Immediately under the handle, and above the space given to the Sun, are seen a Diamond and a Horseshoe. Next on the left are a Snake twisted round a stick, and a Spade, these being placed over the space given to Saturn.

Following them are a Bell and a Club, seen over the sign of Venus. Next, an Eye and Envelope, above the space given to Jupiter.

Then comes a Cross, with the sign of Pisces, the Fishes, these being over the sign of Mercury.

Next are a Winecup and a Spider above the space of Mars.

Followed by a Cat's Head and a Heart, above the Moon.

Each one of these signs round the brim has a symbolic meaning, though their meaning must also be judged by the position they occupy in the cup.

Now, taking the signs round the brim of the cup, and connecting them with the planetary symbols beneath.

Beginning at the handle is a Diamond, this being a token of wealth, which, with the sign of the Sun below, indicates much prosperity, favours, and general well-being, the Horseshoe over the Sun also betokening good luck and successful projects.

In the next space, reading to the left, is the Snake twisted round a stick, over the sign of Saturn. This is indicative of a risk of poverty coming through deceit, and with a Spade over Saturn, whose characteristic is privation, there is a further indication of toil, loss, undoing.

The next sign is a happier one; the Bell over the sign of Venus, with the Club beyond, indicates joyful news, events meaning much happiness, love and peace, the characteristic of Venus being peace or placidity.

Next is the sign of Jupiter, whose characteristic is expansion; above it are placed an Eye and an Envelope, the Eye showing the power of penetration, seeing things in a right perspective, and light thrown on difficult questions, the letter showing that news from all parts of the world is made possible by its expansion.

Next come the Latin Cross and the watery sign Pisces, the Fishes. These being in connection with Mercury, whose characteristic is activity, show much alertness and desire for knowledge; the Cross meaning obstacles and hindrances in the chosen path, whilst the sign of Pisces denotes interesting news from distant lands, with much desire for travel and exploration.

In the next space the Winecup and Spider, in connection with the sign of Mars, the characteristic of Mars being energy, show the strength, courage, and perseverance needed to carry out a successful career; the Spider being a symbol of concentration, patience, and achievement, whilst the Winecup tells of joy and realised ambition.

Following these signs are the Cat's Head and the Heart, with the Crescent Moon below. The characteristic of the Moon is change, mobility; it is also a symbol of good fortune in the tea-leaves. In combination with the Heart it indicates a romantic love affair. The Cat's Head shows interference by those who are mean and spiteful.

Having learned from this brief explanation the symbols of the "Nelros Cup", the reading of the tea-leaves in relation to those symbols will be easy. For instance, suppose the wife of a sailor to be the consultant. Her husband is on his ship in the North Sea, and she is eagerly awaiting news of him. In the cup she has "turned", the symbol of a letter comes in the watery sign)-(with a large ivy leaf beneath it. Further patience will be necessary, the ivy leaf tells us, as the wished-for letter is still far away. The distance from the handle (the consultant) shows this, also the letter symbol being in the watery sign indicates the fact that it will come from across the sea. The waiting for the news causes a feeling of disappointment and sadness; these will vanish later on, and the waiting be compensated by the happy news that will come in the longed-for letter. This is seen by the tea-leaves which appear on other symbols of the cup.

The form of a man is seen between the signs of the Bell and Club; near this form is the letter "A", the first letter of the consultant's name. Round this initial letter is a well-formed circle; a trident lies at a little distance from it.

Here is evidence of the joyful news coming from her husband, the tea-leaves in the spaces of the Bell and Club making a prediction of the satisfactory news a safe one. The circle round the letter "A" and the symbol of the trident near, enable the seer to prophesy a good promotion, much success and happiness.

This example reading of the "Nelros" cup is a fortunate one. We will now consider one of a less satisfactory character.

The consultant is a widow; opposite the handle of the cup she has "turned" is the Envelope over Jupiter, upon the Envelope tea-leaves forming an Owl are seen, beneath is a small arrow pointing towards the handle. These signs foretell bad news probably coming from a far country; the sign of Jupiter and distance from the handle (the consultant) would show this. The symbol of the Owl indicates the anxiety caused by the arrival of the letter and its news. The arrow pointing towards the handle would show that the matter is personal, and will much affect the consultant.

Upon the sign of Saturn, with an arm stretched towards the Spade above it, is the figure of a man. The characteristic of Saturn being privation, and the Spade being a symbol of toil, it is evident that the figure of the man represents someone related to the consultant for whom the present prospects are very bad. It may well be this man from whom is coming the news in the letter which will cause her so much anxiety.

Fortunately, on the Anchor at the bottom of the cup is a well-formed key. Being in this position, it shows that someone at a distance, having the welfare of the consultant much in their mind, will be the means in the future of helping her out of the difficulties. The key being on the Anchor indicates the security she may feel in the friends, who will be instrumental in giving her happiness and peace of mind.

These two example divinations will illustrate the manner in which the tea-leaves are read in relation to the signs upon the cup. To some it may appear an easier means than that of the ordinary tea-cup.

In any case it is very useful to have an alternative method of foretelling the future. Variety is always acceptable, and for this reason I commend the "Nelros Cup of Fortune" to my readers.

A Dictionary of Symbols

A

Abbey.—A sign of increasing wealth and comfort; you will gain much success in your life.

Ace of Clubs.—This signifies good news through the post.

Ace of Diamonds.—You will be gratified by a good present or sum of money.

Ace of Hearts.—Shows affection and happiness in the home.

Ace of Spades.—A large town or building.

Acorn.—This is a symbol of health, strength and gain through industry, a sowing of which you will see the reaping, a short journey from which there may be great results; good fortune and ease are predicted by several acorns.

Aircraft.—If flying towards consultant, hasty news or an unexpected journey; if stationary it gives warning that you will have but little success in your life unless you come out of the rut into which you have fallen.

Albatross.—If seen with the sign of a ship or water it portends distress for those at sea; to sailors or to those associated with them it is an omen of sadness, meaning sorrow and sometimes death.

Alderman (Noble).—To workers this is a sign that if they proceed with caution they will become prosperous.

Alligator.—This is a bad sign of personal danger and distress possibly caused by those nearest to you; it also shows much mental disturbance and worry; if very near consultant a catastrophe is imminent.

Almonds.—These denote festivities and social enjoyment, good and generous friends.

Altar.—If with a figure near, sorrow and distress are foreshown.

Anchor.—A pleasing symbol of good and loyal friends, constancy in love, and the realisation of your wishes; an emblem of safety to a sailor.

Anemone.—These flowers often indicate an event to be expected in the early autumn; the nature of it must be judged by other signs in the cup.

Angel.—This is a symbol of good fortune in love, radiance, happiness, and peace.

Angel (Flying).—A token of love and joy which are swiftly approaching you.

Antlers.—An accident is predicted by this symbol.

Anvil.—Your strength and energy will bring you much success in new plans or enterprises.

Ape.—This animal points to the fact that you have a secret enemy; it denotes malicious and dangerous persons whose tongues are to be feared; it is also a sign of despondency, care, anxiety, and fraud.

Apples.—A pleasant sign of happiness, cheerful conditions, good health, and fortune.

Apple Trees.—These predict a happy event in the apple season.

Apron.—Near consultant brings a new friend; at a distance new work or acquaintances.

Arch.—Things which you desire are developing in the wished-for direction; the arch is a sign of hope; your ambition may be gratified in a most unexpected manner. See also **Triumphal Arch**.

Ark.—This symbol assures you of security and of finding refuge in times of distress and turmoil.

Arm.—If curved, it signifies love, protection, care and strength; stretched out, that a new influence will come into your life which will prove to be an endless source of joy and love.

Armour.—A suit of armour foretells that you will be called upon to face difficulties and dangers and that you will come through them with courage. See **Knight in Armour**.

Arrow.—Unpleasant news or a disagreeable letter from the direction in which it comes.

Artichoke.—This signifies sadness, disappointment and delay; sometimes a secret trouble is indicated by this symbol.

Artist.—To see an artist at work, indicates association with those who study art; also a happy nature finding much joy and beauty in life.

Artist's Mahl Stick.—This implies an artistic temperament, a dislike of daily duties or irksome tasks, and a fretting under any routine; a lack of attention to detail is also a usual characteristic of this symbol.

Arum Lily.—This flower stands for dignity, expectancy, and calm; its fuller meanings must be judged by other symbols around it.

Ass.—If its head is towards consultant, a piece of good news or an event which has long been waited for is near; if its tail, then further patience is necessary, for there will be delay; if it gallops, it gives warning that if people allow themselves to become too boring their friends may reasonably, be expected to avoid them.

Asters.—These flowers indicate a smooth though possibly a somewhat monotonous life; they also show a settled state of mind and sound judgment; if seen in the form of a wreath a death is predicted.

Automatic (Industrial) Machine.—This signifies a lack of initiative and consequent failure in arriving at any great achievement.

Axe.—This shows mastery and power to overcome difficulties; sometimes separation.

B

Baby.—A naked baby near consultant is a sign of sadness and disappointment caused by those who are nearest and dearest; to some it is a sign of money worries; a baby in arms means reconciliation.

Bacon.—Pieces of bacon signify good luck and profitable business.

Badger.—For a maid, or a bachelor, this symbol predicts a single life, but one of freedom, health and success; for the married, it implies regret that they did not remain unmarried.

Bagpipes.—This symbol gives warning of coming sorrow or much agitation and disturbance.

Ball.—See **Football**.

Ballet Dance.—This is a forecast of unsuccessful plans.

Balloon.—A symbol which indicates that much is attempted but little achieved; there is a passing enthusiasm for various experiments and new ideas, but the interest soon flags, and finally vanishes as the balloon in the clouds.

Bananas.—These promise gratification and the occurrence of those things which are most pleasing to you; also a prediction of much happiness and success in love affairs.

Banner.—This is a symbol of a prosperous life.

Barber.—This signifies the approach of a new interest coming into your life, which will lead you to be most particular as to your personal appearance.

Barrel.—Festivity, possibly a picnic; several barrels, prosperity.

Basin.—This symbol stands for small ailments and minor worries; a broken basin, domestic annoyance.

Basket.—Domestic duties and family cares; if full, a present given or received.

Basket of Flowers.—Happiness and contentment, fulfilled desires.

Bassoon.—This musical instrument implies that your energy is apt to exceed your wit.

Bat.—See **Cricket Bat**.

Bath.—This indicates grief or dismay.

Bats.—An ill omen showing sickness and trouble in the home; with other signs, a prediction of death.

Bayonet.—A sign to be feared; it shows danger of operation, wounds, and pain.

Beans.—These show quarrels and disputes with relations.

Bear.—A journey north, sometimes prolonged travel. See also **Polar Bear**.

Bed.—A visit, illness; or death, according to other symbols.

Beef.—A round of beef foretells coming financial worries.

Beehive.—This is a symbol of eloquence, mental capacity, and much energy in forming new schemes and carrying them through; also of attainment to power and honour.

Bees.—These foretell success through your own ability, many friends and enjoyment of life to the full. See also **Bumble Bee**.

Beetle.—This signifies unrest, domestic tribulation, or disagreements; several beetles, that there is a risk of slander and abuse by those whom you regard as friends.

Beetroot.—This symbol indicates that someone will try to do you a bad turn, but it will fail in its object and rather turn out as a benefit.

Bell.—Amazing news according to other signs in the cup; several bells indicate a wedding. See also **Canterbury Bells, Diving Bell, Handbell**.

Belladonna Lily.—This flower is a sign of hope, love, happiness, and the leading of an upright and honourable life.

Bellows.—These show an endeavour to make the best of a bad business.

Besom (Broom).—This gives a caution to avoid meddling in other people's affairs or you may find yourself regarded as an unpleasant busybody.

Bier.—A symbol of death; if near consultant, a personal sorrow, otherwise of a less personal nature.

Billiard table.—Pleasure followed by regret.

Bird Feeding Young.—After a time of patient waiting, your desires will be fulfilled.

Bird of Paradise.—Difficulties and trials are vanishing and a future of comfort and pleasure awaits you.

Bird on a Perch.—If near consultant, news resulting in pleasant plans; if at some distance, there is a doubt of the news being sent.

Birds.—These are significant of happiness and joyful tidings; a single bird flying means speedy news, telegrams (e-mails); birds in a row on a branch or line show that there will be vexatious delay in receiving some wished-for news; birds in a circle denote cogitation followed by swift decision. See also **Clapper for Scaring Birds** and **Stuffed Birds**.

Birds in Cage.—This implies that a variety of causes prevents you from obtaining your dearest wish; should the cage door be open, obstacles will shortly be removed and great happiness will be yours.

Bird's Nest.—This signifies a happy discovery, leading to a fortunate enterprise brought about to a great extent by your own patience and ability; it is also a good omen of love, friends, and increase of fortune.

Biscuits.—These seen in various shapes and sizes foretell the occurrence of pleasant events.

Bishop.—A sign of benevolence, authority, and progress; in cope and mitre, preferment and honour.

Bluebells.—These indicate that an event bringing you much satisfaction and pleasure may be expected to take place in the spring.

Bluebottle Fly.—Unpleasantness and jealousy will be aroused by your success.

Boar.—This animal shows much energy and push though not always in the right direction to bring you unqualified success; it is also a sign of obstacles in your path.

Boat.—Success in a new enterprise; seen with clouds, troubles and disappointment. See also **Ferryboat**.

Bomb.—This foretells a personal disaster or news of an explosion and loss of life.

Bones.—These are an indication of misfortune surmounted with courage.

28

Bonnet.—This implies that youth will be past before you have the best happiness of your life. See also **Widow's Bonnet**.

Book.—An open book shows a desire for information and a mind ever on the alert to understand new theories and facts; a closed book is a sign of expectancy.

Bookcase.—This is a pleasing symbol of coming success through study and perseverance.

Boomerang.—This sign means news from Australia, or that some unexpected development will lead to your having a great interest in that country; with signs of travel, that you will make your home there.

Boots.—These show fortunate business, a good income, and the gratification of your tastes and pleasures; boots of a curious shape foretell an unfortunate enterprise ending in failure.

Boot-tree.—A lucky surprise.

Border.—See **Flower Border**.

Bottle.—A sign of happy days; several bottles indicate extravagant tastes; small bottles, illness.

Bouquet.—This is a most fortunate symbol of coming happiness, love, fulfilled hope, and marriage.

Bow.—A sign of reunion after absence or estrangement.

Bow and Arrow.—This denotes that there is unpleasant talk of your personal affairs which may do you harm.

Bower.—Happiness in love is proclaimed by this symbol.

Box.—An open box foreshows a troubled love affair; a closed box, that you will find something which you had lost.

Boy.—This symbol must be read in accordance with other signs in the cup.

Bracelet.—A discovery made too late.

Branch.—A large branch is a sign of much independence and of success in carrying out an undertaking; the larger it is the greater your success; a broken branch signifies an attempt to organise a project or new scheme which will end in failure.

Bread.—A loaf of bread is a sign of the commonplace and of monotony; several loaves give warning against waste and extravagance, for a shortage of corn is threatened; loaves of bread with crossed swords above them predict mutiny and disaffection among those whom the world trusted.

Bricklayer's Trowel.—A task which you have in hand will be successfully carried out.

Bricks.—These signify new plans and enterprises which will lead to prosperity.

Bride.—This sign indicates a wedding, coming joy, or a rival in your affections, according to other symbols around it.

Bridge.—An advantageous opportunity; a fortunate journey. See also **Suspension Bridge**.

Bridle.—This points to the fact that you greatly object to interference or authority, and that you will always be "top dog" with your friends.

Brooch.—This indicates that you are likely to make a discovery greatly to your advantage, and may in time turn it to good account in the development of a patent; a brooch with dots around it predicts a present.

Broom.—This signifies that there is need for you to be careful in the choice of your friends, and to avoid rushing into an intimacy which you might later have cause to regret.

Bubbles.—See **Child Blowing Soap Bubbles**.

Buckles.—These foretell that some important arrangement of much personal advantage will fall through in an unforeseen manner, causing disappointment and dismay.

Buffalo.—A most unexpected and unusual happening, possibly causing agitation and uncertainty as to the best way to proceed.

Bugle.—This shows a desire for admiration and notice from all whom you meet; it also implies that it is high time to arouse yourself and become more energetic and industrious.

Building.—A sign of removal.

Bull.—An ill omen of misfortune, attacks of pain, or of slander by some enemy; if it gallops with tail up, personal danger or illness of someone dear to you.

Bumble Bee.—This shows a cheerful disposition, making the best of everyone and everything, easily gratified tastes and pleasures; many friends and social success; with other signs, travel is indicated.

Buns.—These signify social amusements and duties, also that you usually take a cheery view of things even in troublesome circumstances.

Buoy.—This is a symbol of hope; you have a good friend in all weathers.

Bush.—Invitations and social enjoyments.

Butter.—This signifies good fortune and success, the comforts of life, and a desire for the best of everything.

Butterfly.—Passing pleasure, power of attraction, many admirers, and flirtations; to the lover it speaks of inconstancy.

Buttonhook.—An exchange between friends, successfully organised plans, and a propitious meeting.

Buttons.—If of various size and shape they mean that there will be many suggestions as to arrangements and new plans without anything definite being settled.

C

Cab.—A sign of gloom, sadness and parting.

Cabbage.—This symbol points out that in spite of thrift and diligence, you will never be very rich.

Cabinet.—An unexpected and fortunate discovery, giving you much pleasure and satisfaction, possibly wealth and unthought-of prosperity.

Cage.—An empty cage shows that you expect to find all manner of amiable qualities in others which are entirely lacking in yourself. See also **Birds in Cage**.

Cakes.—New friends, social success, invitations, and hospitality. See also **Wedding Cake**.

Calf.—This signifies a need for gentleness and kindness to those with whom you associate.

Camel.—A responsibility satisfactorily carried out; sometimes frustrated plans and endless delays; a camel laden means wealth from an unexpected source abroad.

Camera.—This proclaims the fact that you are too fond of gathering new or clever ideas from others, with a view to passing them off as your own original thoughts whenever the opportunity arises.

Campanulas.—These flowers indicate that your hope is centred on one desire, and assure you of the certainty of obtaining your wish.

Candle.—This is significant of trials, worries, or illness.

Candle Extinguisher.—An uncomfortable incident or episode which will put you out considerably.

Candlestick.—You have need to look at things from a wider point of view; to make the best of yourself you must cultivate perception.

Cannon.—This denotes military and naval display and good fortune; with pleasant symbols around or near, such as a crown or star, promotion for someone dear to you in the service.

Canoe.—This implies that a new friendship will eventually lead to a happy love affair.

Canopy.—This brings success through the help and interest of those who are socially or mentally your superiors.

Canterbury Bells.—These graceful flowers indicate that your happiness is to a great extent dependent upon others; if the figure of a woman appeared beside the flowers it will be through a woman that your best happiness comes, if a man were seen it will be one of the male sex to whom you must look for your chief joy in life.

Cap.—This warns you to be cautious in your dealings with those of the opposite sex; it also points to the fact that those things which you desire to hide will become known. See also **Peaked Cap**.

Capstan.—To those associated with the sea, this symbol gives warning of storms; to others, it predicts association with sailors or yachtsmen.

Carafe.—A pleasure which will depend entirely upon yourself is the meaning of this symbol.

Caravan.—This signifies an independent nature, desiring to live a roaming life free of restrictions; should a horse be harnessed to the caravan your ambitions will be fulfilled.

Cards.—See **Ace of Clubs, Ace of Diamonds, Ace of Hearts, Ace of Spades**.

Carnations.—These sweet-scented flowers bring happiness, faithfulness, love, and good friends.

Carpenter at Work.—Necessary arrangement of your affairs is the meaning of this symbol.

Carriage and Horses.-This foretells that your affairs will prosper and that you may reasonably expect the comforts of life; a carriage without horses means that your riches will be transitory, leaving you in poverty; with other signs it denotes that you may be the victim of scandal.

Carrying Chair.—An omen of illness or accident.

Cart.—A symbol of fluctuation in fortune and of a tedious waiting for any settled improvement in financial affairs.

Carving.—Handsome carving is a sign of satisfaction and development.

Castle.—You may expect fortune to smile upon you; a crumbling castle denotes disappointment and ill success in love and marriage.

Cat.—This is an uncomfortable sign of trickery, meanness, and quarrels among relations, money matters probably being the disturbing cause; a cat jumping shows worries and difficulty.

Caterpillar.—You are likely to be criticized unkindly by those who are envious of you, although you have no suspicion that these people are anything but friendly in their feeling towards you; there is slyness and deception, and it would be well to be on your guard or you may find unpleasant gossip has been spread about you.

Cathedral.—Prosperity, contentment, and happiness with those whom you love is the meaning of this symbol.

Cattle.—Profitable transactions.

Cauldron.—New opportunities which need careful consideration.

Cauliflower.—This signifies that even your best friends cannot describe you as constant or reliable.

Cave.—Unless you rouse yourself and use a little more push, you are likely to remain in obscurity all your life.

Celery.—A vigorous body and active mind which will preserve the energies of youth to a good old age.

Chain.—An engagement or wedding; an entangled chain means a dilemma which will tax your ingenuity to the utmost; a long, thick chain indicates ties that you wish to undo; a broken one, trouble in store.

Chair.—A small chair shows an arrival; a large one, deliberation over a new plan. See also **Carrying Chair, Rocking Chair**.

Champagne Glass.—This is a symbol of good fortune and delight; to the sick, a good omen of recovery.

Cheese.—A large cheese denotes that you will benefit by the generosity of prosperous friends.

Cherries.—A love affair, happiness, and health, are the meanings of this symbol.

Chessmen.—These announce the fact that you will be troubled by matters which are difficult to adjust to your satisfaction, and you must expect a certain amount of anxiety and worry.

Chestnut Tree.—An event of interest and importance may be expected in the spring.

Chestnuts.—These show determination in carrying out a scheme which you think will benefit you.

Chicken.—This shows new interests and pleasures; if roosting, domestic tribulation; if flying, troublesome matters.

Child.—This is a sign that you will soon be making fresh plans or forming new projects; a child running means bad news or threatened danger; at play, tranquillity and pleasure.

Child Blowing Soap Bubbles.—Occasions of sadness and joy in quick succession.

Child with Dancing Doll.—The gratification of a wish through an entirely unexpected means.

Child with Tambourine.—Pleasure, lightheartedness, coming good news.

Chimney.—Unless you are cautious you will take a false step; a chimney with smoke to be seen means that you are content, and find pleasure in daily routine and a somewhat commonplace life.

Chisel.—A symbol of losses, dismay, and trouble.

Christmas Tree.—This sign indicates that you may expect some special happiness at the Christmas season.

Chrysanthemums.—These beautiful flowers assure you of a long desired hope in connection with someone dear to you which will be realised in the autumn.

Church.—Courage, honour, and tranquillity; a legacy.

Churning.—This is a happy omen for good and successful results in all you undertake; you will be fortunate and will always take a turn in the right direction for your own happiness.

Cigar.—A wealthy friend or lover who will absorb all your thoughts; a broken cigar signifies a disagreeable incident or a quarrel.

Circle.—Money, presents, an engagement, faithful friends.

Clapper for Scaring Birds.—This sign proclaims that you are offended at small faults or failings in others, and are always eager to bring them into notice, but are blind to your own more obvious deficiencies.

Clarionet.—A pleasure which will be gratified in an unlooked-for manner.

Claw.—This symbol foretells scandal or evil influence.

Clenched Hand.—Indignation; disputes.

Clergyman.—Reconciliation in a long-standing feud.

Clock.—A sign that you desire to hurry over the present and arrive at a time to which you are looking forward.

Clouds.—These denote disappointment, failure of plans, and dismay.

Clover.—A very lucky sign of coming good fortune.

Cloves.—This symbol proclaims the desire for appreciation and the wish to appear at your best on all occasions.

Clown.—Your folly is apparent to everyone.

Clubs.—See **Golf Clubs, Ace of Clubs**.

Coach.—If with horses, you may look forward to a time of ease and luxury; if without horses, it warns you against an act of folly or a harmful indiscretion.

Coal.—Prosperity and good fellowship

Coal-Scoop.—This signifies domestic difficulties or vexation at the turn things have taken.

Coal Scuttle (Bucket).—You will adapt yourself to unaccustomed circumstances requiring much energy.

Coat.—Sadness caused through a parting; if the coat is ragged, distressing news; without sleeves, failure in a new undertaking.

Cobbler.—This predicts a life of arduous and ill-paid work, poor health, and a struggle to make both ends meet.

Cobra.—A warning of grave danger to you or yours.

Cock.—A sign of forthcoming good news, of conquest and triumph.

Cockatoo.—This bird indicates disturbance in the home and some vexation with friends.

Cockchafer (Maybug, Doodlebug).—This predicts a bad harvest season; flying, the arrival of sudden news of a somewhat disagreeable nature.

Cocoanut.—Travel or interesting discoveries.

Coffee Pot.—Dependence on creature comforts; slight indisposition.

Coffin.—A bad omen of coming bereavement; a coffin with a sword beside it shows death of a soldier; with a flag, that of a sailor; with snowdrops, death of a child or infant.

Collar.—Perseverance in the face of obstacles will bring you a great reward.

Collar-Stud.—A reminder of some tiresome or disagreeable little duty which you would fain forget.

Columbine.—These flowers foretell the renewal of a former friendship which is brought about by means of an unthought-of meeting.

Comb.—You will find out that your confidence in someone was misplaced and this discovery will cause you much distress.

Comet.—Favourable weather; unusual and interesting events; to lovers it is an unfavourable omen of separation and blighted hope.

Compasses.—This sign implies that you may expect to travel and to spend your life in interesting activities.

Concertina.—This symbol proclaims dilatory habits and feeble wit.

Conductor.—See **Music Conductor**.

Convolvuli (Bindweeds).—This flower shows feelings of sadness; love and hope which have lasted but a short time now leave only memories to which you cling.

Corks.—This sign shows the power of adapting yourself to your company, and of proving yourself useful in awkward situations.

Corkscrew.—This denotes that you will be vexed by inquisitive people who trouble you with questions.

Cormorant.—This bird is a symbol of agility, swift decisions, and the attainment of your ambition through the power of rapid thought and work.

Corn.—This is a pleasant omen of wealth and success.

Cornucopia.—This symbol predicts great happiness and unqualified success.

Cover.—See **Meat Cover**.

Cow.—A calm, contented state of mind, peaceful and prosperous days.

Cowslips.—A sign of joy; to the married it foretells a birth.

Crab.—Strife, family disagreements, an enemy.

Cradle.—A birth; a broken cradle, sorrow or anxiety about a child.

Crane.—Heavy burdens and anxiety are indicated by this symbol.

Crests.—These are often to be seen and must to some extent be read in connection with other signs in the cup; large crests indicate news of, or communications with, those in positions of authority; small crests, interesting family developments.

Cricket Bat.—A love of sport and a keen desire for fair play in all matters.

Crinoline.—This predicts that unless you retrench in your expenditure, you will have but a pittance to spend upon your dress.

Crocuses.—These flowers are an emblem of joy, and of radiant happiness in love.

Croquet Mallet.—A cheerful and patient disposition, always making the best of things, is the meaning of this symbol.

Cross.—You must expect to meet with hindrances and obstacles in the way of your desires; sorrow and misfortune are also indicated by this symbol. See also **Maltese Cross**.

Crossed Keys.—A sign of authority, power and honour, and an assurance of comfort and help in times of difficulty or doubt.

Crown.—Advancement and honour; the attainment of your highest ambition.

Crutches.—This is an unpleasant sign of forthcoming illness or accident which causes lameness for the time being.

Cucumber.—A new plan successfully carried out.

Cup.—A large cup tells of a splendid opportunity coming your way which will ensure your future success; a small cup means that a little anxiety is before you.

Cupboard.—Disappointment in money affairs.

Curtain.—This symbol proclaims that someone is hiding a matter from you which it would be to your advantage to learn; with other signs

in the cup which are good you may conclude that the matter will be
revealed to you shortly.

Custard Glasses.—A signal of illness, possibly chicken pox or measles.

Cypress.—This tree indicates that you bravely face a difficulty, and finally
overcome it by your own endeavours.

D

Daffodils.—A long-desired hope is about to come to pass, or a delightful
holiday spent in the company of those most congenial to you.

Dagger.—If near and pointing towards consultant, it would be a bad sign
of danger from wounds or an operation; if more distant, it shows a
much less personal danger.

Dahlias.—A sign of some important event which you may expect to take
place in the autumn; it also denotes thrift and increase of fortune.

Daisies.—These imply that you have an attractive, child-like nature, finding
happiness in simple pleasures; a circle of daisies means that you
attract someone to you of the same nature as yourself who will
become all the world to you.

Damsons.—These denote complication of your affairs.

Dance.—See **Ballet Dance**.

Dancer.—A pleasant omen of coming pleasure and gratification, good
news, happiness in love and friendship; it also means that you will
receive an unexpected invitation; several figures dancing in happy
abandonment foretell that your hopes and desires will be fulfilled,
and that many changes will occur, all tending to your success and
future happiness.

Dancing Doll.—See **Child with Dancing Doll**.

Dandelion.—Unexpected news of the marriage of an old friend whom you
had always supposed would never marry.

Dates.—A pleasure which is unlikely to come up to your expectations is
the meaning of this symbol.

Deer.—An unfortunate indication that your ventures in new directions of work or business will end in failure; if running, a fruitless endeavour to undo your past mistakes; a dead deer, that you will be the innocent cause of distress to someone you love.

Desk.—You will receive a letter which will upset you, or you will lose the friendship of someone with whom you have corresponded regularly for many years.

Devil.—This symbol gives warning that reformation is needed, or you may find yourself so tightly in the grip of bad influence that it will be well-nigh impossible to extricate yourself.

Diadem.—This ensign of royalty shows that your ambition is realised beyond your expectations; wonderful good fortune and influential friends assure you of an unusually successful career.

Diamonds.—See **Ace of Diamonds**.

Dish.—Anxiety in household matters; a broken dish is a foretaste of a greater loss.

Diver.—A great and unexpected piece of news which will lead to a fortunate discovery; to the lover, it reveals deception.

Diving Bell.—This sign predicts that you may one day find yourself in danger on the sea or river.

Dog.—This symbol has many meanings which must be read in accordance with the other symbols; in a general way this sign indicates adverse conditions, the thwarting of life's chances, unfortunate love affairs, family misfortune and money troubles; a large dog sometimes signifies protection and good friends; a small dog, vexation and impatience.

Doll.—A festivity at which you will endeavour to conceal your feelings of boredom under somewhat foolish hilarity. See also **Child with Dancing Doll, Rag Doll**.

Dolphin.—A cheerful and optimistic character, pleasure on the sea or river.

Dovecot.—Peace in the home.

Doves.—These birds give a personal message of happiness and an assurance of faithfulness in love, peaceful circumstances, high ideals, and progress; to those who are at enmity this symbol proclaims reconciliation; to the sick or anxious, comfort and hope; to a business man, a fortunate omen of success.

Dragon.—Great and sudden changes about which there is an element of danger.

Dragon-Fly.—Tidings of unexpected occurrences, unlooked-for events, new and advantageous opportunities, sometimes new clothes or furniture.

Drum.—A hazardous enterprise or expedition is the meaning of this symbol.

Drummer.—To a man, this foreshows popularity and a successful public career; to a woman, social success, a large following of friends and admirers, and power of gaining her own ends.

Duck.—A sign of a taste for speculation; if more than one duck, success in work and enterprise, profitable undertakings.

Dumb Bell.—A chance meeting which will lead to the making of a new friend.

Dustpan and Brush.—You will be certain to hear of domestic tribulation amongst your friends or relatives; if this symbol appears in your cup with other signs of vexation, it would indicate personal domestic annoyance.

E

Eagle.—This predicts that you may expect most beneficial changes, the realisation of a long-cherished hope, and possibly an inheritance of wealth from an unexpected source; a flying eagle shows the coming of wealth and honour after a change of residence; with a vulture, death of a monarch; a dead eagle, public loss and mourning.

Eagle's Nest.—An eagle on its nest foretells association with those in places of authority and honour; it also denotes a life of wealth and ease.

Ear.—A large ear shows that you will be shocked by hearing of some scandal or abuse; a normal ear means that you will receive some interesting and pleasant piece of news or valuable information.

Ear-rings.—To a man this symbol proclaims the displeasure of one of the opposite sex; to a woman, the humiliation of unrequited affection.

Earwig.—A sign of uncomfortable discoveries in the home, troubles with domestics, deceit and prying.

Easel.—A sign of marriage to widows and maids; to the married, increase of worldly goods; this symbol must be read in connection with other indications in the cup.

Eels.—This is an unpleasant symbol meaning malicious tongues and treacherous friends, also gossip over money matters.

Egg Cup.—A sign of an escape from a threatened disaster.

Eggs.—New plans and ideas, or a birth.

Elephant.—A sign of power, travel, promotion, happiness and stability in love and friendship.

Elf.—This symbol should put you on your guard or you may be the victim of an unpleasant practical joke.

Elm Tree.—A good omen of prosperity and coming happiness.

Emu.—Lack of caution will not be one of your failings.

Engine (Train).—Journeys, trouble on the railway, strikes, accident, and hasty news are the meanings of this symbol.

Ensign.—See **Flag**.

Escape.—See **Fire Escape**.

Extinguisher.—See **Candle Extinguisher**.

Eye.—This signifies penetration and the solving of difficulties; it also shows depth of character and love.

Eyeglasses.—You will make a beneficial discovery through surprising means.

F

Faces.—Several of these denote an invitation to a party or wedding; ugly faces mean disturbances or bad news; pretty faces, pleasure and love; two faces upon one head, looking diverse ways, indicate that you may hear yourself accused of deception and falseness, or that these things may be practised upon you; a bearded face, health and strength, but an indolent nature, which is a source of vexation to those around you.

Falcon.—This bird warns you to be on your guard, for you have an enemy.

Fan.—Love of admiration, frivolity, pleasure with the opposite sex.

Fate.—This is indicated by a straight thin line of tea leaves which ascends towards the consultant; what may be expected of fate must be judged by the line itself and other signs in the cup.

Feathers.—Large feathers signify achievement and prosperity; to authors, literary success; small feathers denote something of which you are afraid, but which you will meet with courage.

Feet.—You will be called upon to take a decisive step in some matter which may lead up to an eventful change in your life.

Fence.—This means that there is but a step between you and success.

Fender.—You will constantly come in contact with someone to whom you feel a strong antipathy.

Ferns.—Dignity, peace, and steadfast love are the meanings of this symbol.

Ferret.—Jealousy and enmity are likely to cause you distress.

Ferry-Boat.—This symbol implies that difficulties will be smoothed away for you by the aid of good and useful friends.

Field Marshal's Hat.—To a soldier, or those who are associated with them, this is a sign of coming promotion, triumph, and of the attainment to honour.

Figs.—These indicate joy and abundance of the good things of this world; to those in business it is an omen of success and prosperity.

Figurehead of a Ship.—A good omen for your future Welfare; this symbol predicts that you will be enabled to steer your course through smooth waters.

Figures.—See **Numbers, Human Figures, Running Figures**.

Finger.—This usually indicates a special need for attention to be paid to adjoining symbols.

Fire Engine.—An evidence of a serious fire of which you will hear or from which you will suffer; this must be judged by other indications in the cup.

Fire Escape.—An urgent warning to take all precautions against fire.

Fireplace.—Your chief interests in life will probably lie in your home; small duties, simple pleasures, and a circle of friends.

Fish.—News from abroad; with other signs of movement, emigration; a starfish is a sign of good luck.

Flag.—Danger, rebellion, and war are the meanings of this symbol.

Flower-Border.—That for which you have long hoped and waited is about to come to pass.

Flowers.—Many pleasant meanings may be given to this symbol, good fortune, happiness, love, marriage, and a large circle of admiring friends, being among them. See also **Basket of Flowers, Foxgloves, Lily, Forget-me-not**.

Fly.—This signifies small vexations and annoyances which will ruffle you considerably. See also **Bluebottle Fly, Dragon Fly**.

Font.—News of a birth or an invitation to a christening party.

Foot.—This indicates a journey; a swollen foot, injury, or news of an accident to the foot.

Football.—Love of outdoor games, or a keen interest in the welfare of those who take part in them, is shown by this symbol.

Forge.—This implies a need for refinement and of reconstructing your ideas on many subjects.

Forget-me-not.—This flower speaks of the attainment of a cherished hope, also that you will probably find your truest happiness in love and marriage.

Fork.—This warns you against those who constantly flatter you; it would be well for you to be on your guard or you may one day awake to the fact that all this flattery was used as a tool to harm you.

Fountain.—A most favourable omen foretelling happiness, success in love and marriage, prosperity in business, and good fortune in all you undertake; this symbol also points to an unexpected legacy.

Fox.—This denotes that you may have an unsuspected enemy, possibly disloyal dependents; sometimes it means theft and trickery.

Foxgloves.—These show ambition and attainment; if broken or bending, defeated plans and hopes.

Frog.—A change of residence; with other signs, new work or profession; with bad symbols around, unpleasant sights and stories.

Fruit.—A happy sign of forthcoming prosperity and general advancement.

G

Gaiters.—Your chief interests will be in outdoor work and amusements; intellectual pursuits will not attract you; to clergy, or to those associated with them, gaiters indicate promotion.

Gallows.—An omen of great distress and tragedy.

Garden Roller.—An indication that things around you are liable to become somewhat unmanageable, and that you will need tact and strength to avoid being crushed by circumstances.

Garland.—A sign of happiness, love and honour.

Garters.—A contempt for feminine weakness is the meaning of this sign.

Gate.—An excellent opportunity awaits you, perhaps the chance of a lifetime; massive high gates denote restriction, misery, or imprisonment.

Geese.—These indicate the arrival of unexpected and rather troublesome visitors.

Gentian.—A memory which is interwoven with sorrow and joy.

Geranium.—This flower shows a strong will and determined character, contentment, and happiness; it also denotes two opposite natures who have a great bond of affection between them.

Giant.—There is, or will be, a serious obstacle in your path.

Giraffe.—You are apt to cause mischief through blundering and the making of incorrect statements.

Gladioli.—These flowers indicate courage in the face of difficulty; hope and tenderness.

Glasses.—These show that you will entertain your friends on a lavish scale, and delight in hospitality, but will occasionally be confronted by difficulties in your arrangements. See also **Champagne Glass, Custard Glasses, Eyeglasses, Hand Glass**.

Gleaner (Gatherer).—You will always endeavour to make the best of the circumstances in which you find yourself but will seldom possess the most desirable things in life.

Goat.—A new enterprise which has an element of risk about it; a goat is an unfortunate sign to sailors or to those connected with them.

Golf Clubs.—These indicate a life so full of work that there is but little leisure for recreation.

Gondola.—A visit to Italy, or a romance are the meanings of this sign.

Gong-and-Stick.—This symbol warns you to expect little else than the "trivial round and common task" for the present.

Goose.—A venture needing much discussion and arrangement; plans are made only to be upset again, and unless you proceed with caution, you are likely to make a bad mistake.

Gramophone.—This usually portends vexation at being drawn into a somewhat disorderly and noisy pleasure.

Grapes.—These signify pleasure, abundance, fulfilment, and a life free from care.

Grasshoppers.—These insects give warning of a poor harvest season; for an old person the risk of chill leading to severe illness.

Grave.—This symbol must be read in accordance with its position, also with reference to other signs in the cup; as a general rule, with gloomy signs it would bring a message of coming sorrow, or with cheerful symbols that a death would benefit the consultant.

Greyhound.—This sign stands for energy and untiring activity which will bring you unqualified success; it also denotes that you may expect favourable tidings of the result of a new enterprise.

Grindstone.—The aftermath of an indiscretion.

Guitar.—This symbol displays strong power of attraction for the opposite sex, also pleasant adventures ending in a happy love affair.

Gun.—A very disquieting symbol, grave danger of a sudden calamity; with other bad signs, a violent death.

H

Hammer.—Troublesome little tasks which you are reluctant to undertake.

Hammock.—A mournful ending of something to which you had looked forward with delight.

Ham with Frill.—This denotes a nice invitation, hospitality, pleasure with your friends; also enjoyment followed by dismay; a ham without a frill means increasing fortune and success.

Hand.—A sign of good fellowship, loyalty, and affection; it may also indicate a parting, a meeting or a bargain concluded; other signs around it must be noticed in order to read its special meaning. See also **Clenched Hand**.

Handbell.—You would much like to startle the world by a wonderful discovery or amazing theory by which your name would be known for all time but you will need every possible good symbol to appear in the cup to give you any assurance of your ambition being gratified.

Handcuffs.—Disgrace, imprisonment, misfortune, and dishonesty; this sign must be read in connection with others around it.

Handglass.—An illusion quickly dispelled is the meaning of this symbol.

Handscreen.—Even small demands sometimes necessitate great effort on the part of those to whom the demand is made.

Hare.—The return of an absent friend after a long absence; if it is running, a journey is indicated; a dead hare foreshows money acquired through industry.

Harebell.—Peace, a placid existence, and faithfulness in love are the meanings of this lovely little flower; with other signs you may expect news of a birth.

Harp.—This is a sign of melancholy and predicts the possibility of a nervous breakdown.

Harrissi Lily.—These graceful flowers predict peace, joy, hope, and a wedding.

Harrow.—This shows that much of your time will be given endeavouring to make the lives of those around you smooth and happy, whilst you cheerfully spend your days in a somewhat monotonous manner.

Harvest.—A shock of corn is a somewhat sad emblem showing that you have sown that of which the reaping will be tears; it is also a warning of illness, especially to the aged.

Hastener for Roasting Meat.—You are reminded that you should endeavour to move with the times, and not cling so tenaciously to ideas and habits which are now obsolete.

Hat.—A symbol of luck, presents, success in new work or enterprise; sometimes it foreshows the arrival of a visitor.

Hawk.—This is an unfortunate symbol, as it denotes circumstances in which people and things seem to be working against you, placing you in awkward and embarrassing predicaments.

Hayrick.—This indicates a desire for mastery and preeminence; it also shows that a doubt will arise as to how best to proceed, but you will find the right way out and will come to a wise decision.

Head.—A large head gives warning of family trouble or of serious illness; a very small head, waning ability or power; several heads, mental distress or derangement.

Hearse.—A sign of bereavement or of sad news of those who are bereaved.

Heart.—A sign of coming happiness through the affections bringing joy into your life, or satisfaction through money, according to other signs near.

Hearts.—See **Ace of Hearts**.

Heather.—A most fortunate sign of gratified wishes and of coming good luck; to lovers it is an assurance of much happiness.

Hedge.—This shows that through energy and perseverance you will surmount obstacles and carry all before you.

Hedgehog.—You will be immensely surprised by hearing that someone whom you had always thought of as a confirmed bachelor is about to be married.

Hemlock.—The shadows of your past life have an inconvenient habit of appearing at the most awkward moments.

Hens.—Comfort and domestic felicity; a hen roosting shows domestic annoyance and money worries.

Highlander.—This is a sign of sound business capacity and a plodding contriver in transactions.

Hive.—See **Beehive**.

Hockey Stick.—A keenness for games and success in the playing of them.

Hoe.—This means that you will often have more to do than you can well accomplish; each day things will occur needing your attention and increasing your work, but in spite of it you will have good health and cheerfulness.

Holly.—This indicates that something of importance may be expected to occur in the winter; unless gloomy signs appear in the cup, it may be assumed that the event will be a happy one.

Hollyhock.—You will have a friend, or lover, who will never disappoint you.

49

Honeycomb.—Prosperous undertakings, honour and renown, and much which is delightful are foreshown by this symbol.

Hoop.—You will find immense satisfaction in doing things that require energy even if they are of little importance.

Horns.—You have a powerful enemy, or at least someone who has feelings of animosity towards you, which may prove to be unpleasant in their result.

Horse.—Comforts, loyal friends, and pleasure; galloping horses mean that events are hurrying towards you over which you have no control, bringing many changes into your life. See also **Carriage and Horses**.

Horse Collar.—To those who own horses, or do business with them, this sign is a pleasant indication of success in some transaction; to others it would imply toil and a strenuous effort to keep things going.

Horseman.—See **Mounted Horseman**.

Horseshoe.—An unexpected piece of good fortune, the achievement of your wish, and good luck in all you undertake; a double horseshoe hastens the arrival of your desires; a horseshoe reversed means an upset of plans causing much disappointment and vexation; a broken one denotes a dilemma, trials, or discomforts.

Hot-Water Bottle.—You will always find compensation in all trials and discomforts.

Hot-Water Can.—Indisposition, irritability, annoyances.

Hourglass.—A warning against delay in arrangements or thought-of plans; with other signs, the hourglass is a grave warning of peril through illness or accident.

House.—A successful transaction, a visit, a new home.

Human Figures.—These must be judged with regard to what they appear to be doing.

Hyacinth.—This flower predicts love, joy, and gratified ambition.

I

Ibex on Rock.—After a time of strenuous effort and struggle, you will achieve triumph and a position of security and peace.

Initials.—These frequently occur, and usually point to names of people from whom you may expect to hear shortly; or they may indicate places.

Inkpot.—Expectancy.

Iris.—These flowers bring a message of hope and pleasure.

Iron.—Small vexations or troubles which will quickly pass, is the meaning of this symbol.

Ivory.—This foretells increased wealth and a well-merited reward for past industry.

Ivy.—Patience, understanding, steadfastness, and loyal friends are indicated by this sign.

J

Jackdaw.—Sagacity, dependable friends, and knowledge acquired by persevering study.

Jam.—Pots of jam caution you against extravagance and waste.

Jelly.—This foreshows a time of pleasure and a time of pain.

Jemmy (Crowbar).—A bad attack of toothache is indicated by this weapon.

Jewellery.—You may expect an increase of wealth, possibly good presents also.

Jockey.—Successful dealing and good money enterprise; luck in racing and speculation.

John Bull.—This figure implies that you are likely to witness, or partake in, an event of national importance.

Judge in Robes.—Legal affairs, personal or otherwise according to other indications in the cup; this sign is often seen during a famous trial or when such is about to take place.

Jug.—This shows good health and money making.

Jumping Figure.—Change which will be greatly to your advantage.

K

Kangaroo.—You will receive an unlooked-for and interesting piece of news; sometimes it indicates that you have a rival.

Kettle.—This is a sign of illness; unless a human figure appears beside it, the illness is probably for the consultant; it is an omen of coming trouble.

Key.—Circumstances will improve, things will become easy, and your path will be made smooth; you may hope for success in whatever you have on hand; a key at some distance from the consultant denotes the need for the assistance of good and influential friends in times of difficulty. See also **Crossed Keys**.

Keyhole.—This gives warning of a need for caution, for someone of whom you feel no suspicion is untrustworthy.

Kingfisher.—This beautiful bird signifies the return of someone for whom you have been longing; if flying, news of a surprising nature will speedily arrive.

King on His Throne.—Security and peace; it may also mean that you gain a high position through influential friends.

Kite.—Vanishing pleasures and benefits, or scandal, are the meanings of this sign.

Kneeling Figure.—A new enterprise or project; care should be taken to think it over well; do nothing rashly and seek reliable advice.

Knife.—This is an unpleasant sign of quarrels, broken friendship, and tears.

Knight in Armour.—This sign predicts good fortune, success in love, and loyalty to your friends.

Knives.—These signify danger of wounds, attacks of pain, and dismay.

L

Laburnum Tree.—A sign of delight and the fulfilment of a cherished hope, probably occurring in the spring.

Ladder.—This signifies advancement, influential friends, and the attainment of good fortune.

Lamb.—An indication that you will be amazed by the success of a doubtful undertaking. See also **Prancing Lamb.**

Lamp.—This sign provides an assurance of good success in business. See also **Street Lamp.**

Lantern.—This shows that fear and doubt will mar your happiness and progress.

Laurel.—This tree points to power, ability and health.

Leaves.—Prosperous results of your diligence, new friends, and satisfaction.

Leek.—This implies that you are anxious to come to the root of some matter of which at present you have only an inkling; with good signs around, you may expect to come to a satisfactory understanding.

Leg.—This foretells a successful race with fortune.

Leg of Mutton.—Depression and pecuniary worries is the meaning of this sign.

Leopard.—This animal foreshows triumph over adverse circumstances or an evil report; two leopards, fortune and misfortune following each other in quick succession.

Letters.—These are shown by oblong or square tea-leaves, initials near give the name of the writer; with dots around they will contain money.

Lettuce.—This shows sleeplessness, possibly from the receiving of some perturbing news.

Lighthouse.—A good sign of security and of light on your path whenever it is most needed; if crooked or broken, disaster at sea.

Lightning.—Forked lightning seen in a zig-zag up the side of the cup shows bad weather conditions; if near the figure of a man or woman, it may possibly indicate death from lightning or electrical mechanism; if seen at the bottom of the cup and with a clear space indicating water, it would mean bad storms abroad causing damage and loss.

Lilac.—This is an emblem of radiant happiness; joys shared with another, with whom there is perfect oneness of purpose and love.

Lily-of-the-Valley.—A fortunate omen of realisation, love, and marriage. See also **Arum Lily, Belladonna Lily, Madonna Lily, Harrissi Lily, Water Lily**.

Limpets.—These denote that you endeavour to wrest from others some valuable secret which they possess, but without success; limpets are a sign of good luck to fishermen and promise a big haul of fish.

Lines of Dots.—These indicate journeys and their probable length and direction; to be read in connection with other signs of movement; wavy lines mean tiresome journeys or difficulties likely to be encountered; if the lines ascend sharply to the brim of the cup, a journey to a hilly country will be taken.

Lion.—One of the most fortunate symbols indicating high hopes and excellent prospects, association with distinguished persons, honour, and fame.

Lizard.—This suggests treachery and the probability of a plot being laid against you by false and deceitful friends.

Lobster.—A pleasant event, or a good present, is shown by this symbol.

Lock and Key.—You are warned against the loss of something which you value.

Looking Glass.—This implies a desire to know the truth, even if it be unpleasant to you.

Lord Mayor's Coach.—You will receive a good offer from an unexpected quarter.

Lute.—This is a sign of a secret sadness of which those around you know nothing; to musicians, a good omen of success.

Lynx.—To the married a bad omen of estrangement, possibly divorce; to others it denotes treachery or episodes of a painful nature.

M

Macaroni.—This proclaims the sad fact that you must endeavour to make sixpence do the work of a shilling.

Mace.—Promotion, a position of authority and achievement.

Machine.—See **Automatic (Industrial) Machine**.

Madonna Lily.—This flower means perfection and peace, and the assurance of love and truth.

Magnet.—You will be drawn by an irresistible attraction towards someone for whom you will eventually feel more dislike than affection.

Magnifying Glass.—You are given to such exaggeration that it amounts to untruthfulness.

Magnolia.—This tree brings calm and peaceful conditions after a time of unrest.

Magpie.—"One for sorrow, two for mirth, three for a wedding, four for a birth"; this ancient saying well explains the meaning of seeing magpies in the tea-leaves.

Mahl Stick.—See **Artist's Mahl Stick**.

Mallet.—You will arrive at a wise conclusion in a difficult matter. See also **Croquet Mallet**.

Maltese Cross.—You will emerge from one source of vexation or trouble only to fall into another.

Man.—You may expect a visitor.

Man Carrying a Burden.—An unhappy marriage or an unfortunate love affair.

Man Carrying Mace.—This points to personal promotion or the advancement of someone dear to you.

Man Speaking from a Platform.—Public news or developments which will specially interest or concern you.

Marrow.—See **Vegetable Marrow**.

Mars.—This sign will often be seen, and indicates a courageous, energetic nature, fond of exploits and freedom, and shows a capacity for strenuous work; a fortunate symbol for a soldier.

Mask.—For a lover, this predicts that unpleasant facts will come to light, of which at present there is no suspicion, leading to an abrupt ending of the love affair.

Mass of Leaves.—Arrivals and departures about which there are little difficulties.

Mast.—This symbol must be read in connection with the surrounding signs.

Mastiff.—This dog warns you of an unexpected emergency in which there is danger of your being overpowered by the arguments of those who are masterful.

Maypole.—This shows that you find but little satisfaction in your amusements and gaiety; for whilst you appear to enter into them in a light-hearted manner, you are craving for further excitement.

May Tree.—This signifies the receiving of a joyous message.

Meat.—A sign of financial worry.

Meat Cover.—An unpleasant emergency or discovery.

Medal.—You will be rewarded for past industry by future prosperity.

Medicine Bottle.—An unpleasant sign of illness.

Medlar.—This tree predicts a condition of transient happiness.

Meerschaum Pipe.—You will be disturbed by some news from a man who has much influence in your life.

Melon.—This means gratification and good news, and the deriving of much pleasure from the appreciation of those whose good opinion is of value to you.

Mercury.—This planet is constantly seen in the tea-leaves and is a symbol of ceaseless activity of striving to attain great things; it also indicates good business capacity.

Mermaid.—To those associated with the sea, this is a warning of shipwreck or other peril.

Merrythought.—The attainment of a wish or small pleasure.

Mice.—These indicate danger of poverty through fraud or theft.

Milk Cans.—These show an agricultural enterprise that will be to your advantage.

Milk Churn.—A good emblem of future comfort and increased happiness.

Milking Stool.—A new venture about which you will feel somewhat dubious but which with care will be carried out successfully.

Mineshaft.—This is a hopeful sign of coming peace after a time of discontent amongst miners, or a coal strike.

Mirror.—Prophetic dreams; a love of truth.

Mistletoe.—This signifies that a cherished hope is unlikely to be fulfilled, or at any rate it will only be after many months have passed, and when you have become weary of waiting.

Mitre.—A prediction of honour and promotion for a clergyman.

Monk.—Religious controversy and disturbances.

Monkey.—This is an unpleasant indication that ugly rumours and scandal will be spread about you or yours; sometimes public notoriety; with other signs, it foreshows grief and pain.

Monkey-on-Organ.—Difficult circumstances and a hard struggle are the meanings of this sign.

Monkey Puzzle Tree.—A task lies before you which you will find hard, but for which you will afterwards be rewarded by meeting with great success.

Monograms.—These will often be found in the tea-leaves and will indicate someone of much importance in your life, whose initials are shown by the monogram.

Monument.—Someone in whose career you are much interested will rise to fame.

Moon.—A crescent moon denotes good news, fortune, and romance; for a man it predicts public recognition and honour.

Mortar.—A sign of gloom, illness, emergencies.

Motor Car.—Short journeys by road or rail, visits from friends; with other signs, some increase of fortune may be expected.

Mountain.—This gives promise of the realisation of a great ambition and of the influence of powerful friends; many mountains indicate obstructions and sometimes powerful enemies in your career.

Mounted Horseman.—A sign of good friends, luck, and advantageous offers.

Mouse.—This invariably indicates that there is need for a trap to be set; it also gives warning that domestic worries are to be expected.

Muff.—This implies caprice and ostentation.

Mug.—This symbol predicts a merry meeting.

Mushroom.—This predicts that you will take a small risk and achieve a great success; to lovers, it foreshows a quarrel and possibly a broken engagement.

Music Conductor.—A good sign to a musician; to others it suggests that enthusiasm and good spirits will carry them through life very happily.

Mutton Chop.—Fruitless discussion or indisposition are the meanings of this sign. See also **Leg of Mutton**.

Myrtle Tree.—This speaks of affection and peace; a declaration of love, and a happy marriage.

N

Nail.—Toothache and painful dentistry are foreshown by this sign.

Names.—To see the name of a person or place, signifies events occurring in connection with such person or place; if good symbols appear, pleasant happenings may be expected; if gloomy signs, then trouble will arise associated with the name seen.

Narcissus.—This flower shows sentiment and coming joy; also that some new idea will unfold itself to you in the spring and will prove to be of much advantage to you.

Necklace.—A good present or money; a broken necklace shows that you will break a bond which you have grown to feel is unendurable.

Needles.—These denote mischief and deceit; sometimes disappointment in love.

Neptune.—This planetary symbol indicates a condition of chaos.

Nest.—See **Bird's Nest, Eagle's Nest**.

Net.—Toil or anxiety followed by amazing achievement and good fortune.

Ninepins.—These show a mind determined to gain success whatever the cost in drudgery.

Nose.—A large nose denotes dissipation; a crooked one shows a wayward and untrustworthy character; a long, thin nose implies that you change your ideas on various subjects and alter your mode of life in accordance with your new ideas.

Nosegay.—See **Bouquet**.

Notice-Board.—Your attention will be called to some fact which it will be to your advantage to learn.

Numbers.—These are frequently found in the tea-leaves, and must be read in conjunction with surrounding symbols. If the consultant has a lucky number, and this appears with good signs, it promises much success. An unlucky number with gloomy signs predicts misfortune. A journey with a five near obviously points out that it will be taken in five days, or weeks, and so on. Ten dots, close together, means ten pounds or shillings, according to the size and number of the dots. Numbers with the symbol of a legacy show the amount to be expected.

Nun.—This is a sign that you will probably remain unmarried through your own choice; to the married it implies unjust suspicion.

Nurse.—A nurse in uniform usually foretells illness for yourself or for someone dear to you.

Nut-Crackers.—This portends that you will strive to solve a difficult problem, the result of which is of much importance to you.

Nuts.—Gratified ambition and wealth are indicated by nuts.

O

Oak Tree.—This is a good omen of wealth, strength, and attainment of cherished hopes; for a lover, it predicts happiness and prosperity in marriage.

Oar.—Sport; amusements; a broken oar denotes recklessness for which you will pay dearly; for a lover or husband, this means affliction.

Obelisk.—This foreshows honour and wealth.

Oil-Can.—Work and worry are foretold by this sign.

Onions.—You may expect that something which you supposed was a secret will be discovered, possibly through treacherous friends.

Opera-Glasses.—You are in danger of losing the confidence of your friends because of your inquisitive questions.

Orchids.—These give a pleasing assurance of coming good fortune and a life of ease and wealth.

Organ.—This must be read in connection with other signs around it; sometimes it means a wedding, death, or realised ambition; to a musician, it is a good omen of achievement. See also **Barrel Organ**.

Ostrich.—This symbol points to achievement in creative work; if running, you may look for startling news and rumours of public upheavals.

Otter.—You must expect to receive a disagreeable shock through some unpleasant spite on the part of those of whom you have always thought well, and regarded as loyal and affectionate friends.

Overcoat.—You may expect to have changes in your life and become of much importance.

Owl.—A bad omen of illness, misfortune, and poverty; if flying, you will receive tidings of grief; to lovers this bird is a symbol of bad news or unpleasant rumours; to those who are contemplating new work or enterprise the owl should be regarded as a warning to proceed with caution.

Ox.—An ox in his stall implies hospitality, domestic peace and abundance.

Oysters.—These are a sign of enjoyment and expensive tastes, also that you will appreciate the pleasures of life more in your later years than in your youthful days.

P

Padlock.—An open padlock means a surprise; a closed one, a need for precaution.

Pagoda.—Foreign travels.

Pail.—You will be called upon to undertake a variety of things which you dislike.

Pails on Yoke.—In the future you may hope for compensation for past trials and weariness.

Palace.—This portends good fortune and favours.

Palette.—A hopeful sign of success to an artist or to those associated with one; to others, it suggests a need for deliberation and advice before embarking upon a new work or enterprise.

Palm Tree.—This is a symbol of honour, fame, and victory; increase of wealth, love, and marriage.

Pampas Grass.—This is a sign that you will make a pathetic endeavour to find happiness in a life which is cast in a somewhat dreary lot.

Pan and His Pipes.—A most cheering symbol which gives an assurance of happiness, future prosperity, and delight.

Pansy.—This flower is a symbol of understanding, modesty, and contentment; it is also a pleasant indication of faithful friends and happy days.

Panther.—You may expect to be shocked at the treacherous behaviour of a friend whom you had always regarded as honourable.

Paradise.—See **Bird of Paradise**.

Parallel Lines.—These predict well-thought-out and smoothly running plans.

Parcels.—These are shown by thick, square or round leaves.

Parrot.—This is a sign of foreign travel, the making of many friends, and much mental energy; sometimes it gives a hint that there is an inclination to gossip and spread scandal.

Parsley.—Small events will bring you satisfaction.

Peacock.—A sign of the acquisition of property; a prosperous and happy marriage; with other signs, an unfortunate friendship.

Peaked Cap.—The arrival of a male visitor.

Pears.—Improved social condition and other advantages; this fruit brings success to a business man and to a woman a rich husband; one pear signifies a birth or new plans.

Pedestrian.—An important appointment or urgent business.

Pelican.—This bird is a symbol of loneliness, separation, and yearning for the unattainable; if it is flying you will receive news from those who are far away in isolated parts of the world.

Pen.—See **Quill Pen**.

Penguin.—This strange bird indicates interesting news of expeditions and discoveries in the northern regions.

Penknife.—This is an unfortunate symbol of enmity, disloyalty, and jealousy.

Peonies.—You will probably be called upon to make a decision of much importance before another summer is past; broken peonies predict that you may possibly throw away your chance of happiness by coming to a wrong conclusion.

Pepper-Pot.—This means vexation and unreasonable irritation which you will endeavour to conceal.

Perambulator.—News of a birth.

Pestle.—A sign of decisive measures; a remedy for a grievance or an ill.

Pheasant.—Good fortune; new friends; if flying, speedy and propitious news.

Piano.—This is a sign that you will make the most of your opportunities and will gain that for which you have aimed; to musicians, a sign of advancement.

Pickaxe.—This sign proclaims labour troubles and strikes.

Pig.—This assures you of gain and success in agricultural interests; it also denotes that you may expect a present of money or a legacy.

Pigeons.—These show reconciliation with someone dear to you from whom you have been estranged; if flying, important and pleasant news is on its way; if stationary, delay in the arrival of important news.

Pillar.—A symbol of strength, protection from danger, and of good and powerful friends; a broken pillar predicts sorrow and despair.

Pincers.—A painful experience; an injury; toothache.

Pincushion.—Thrift, order, and a well-regulated household.

Pineapple.—A pleasing indication of wealth, rich friends, and good presents.

Pine Trees.—Happiness followed by an aftermath of regret.

Pipe.—A visit from a dear friend; several pipes foreshow news from a man who is much in your thoughts. See also **Meerschaum Pipe, Pan and His Pipes**.

Pistol.—An ominous warning of disaster; with other bad signs, of a violent death.

Pitcher.—This shows an endeavour to relieve a rather dull and monotonous life, by throwing your energy into somewhat unnecessary work.

Pitchfork.—A sign that you are apt to stir up feud, and make peace and quiet impossible.

Plate.—For the present, you will merely jog along in an ordinary way.

Playing Cards.—See **Ace of Clubs, Ace of Diamonds, Ace of Hearts**, and **Ace of Spades**.

Plough.—You must expect to go through toil and frustration before you finally conquer your difficulties and achieve triumph.

Plum Pudding.—This denotes festivity and cheerfulness.

Plums.—These foretell a new development of plans.

Polar Bear.—This sign means a journey to a cold climate.

Policeman.—This tells you to beware of theft and underhand practices; with other signs, it would indicate trouble probably caused by those with whom you are most closely associated.

Pope.—Unexpected gain and future happiness are foretold by this sign.

Poppy.—This flower is significant of a pleasant occurrence in the early summer.

Porter and Truck.—This indicates a pending journey or the arrival of a traveller.

Post.—This signifies a formidable obstacle; if broken, that you will encounter a storm of opposition to your plan.

Postman.—Important and profitable news.

Pot.—See **Coffee Pot**.

Potato.—You will have need of patience in your daily life, and will sometimes be troubled by pecuniary difficulties.

Prancing Lamb.—This is a symbol of trouble which will have beneficial results and will lead to contentment and happiness.

Prawns.—These bring pleasures, presents and satisfactory arrangements.

Prince of Wales' Plumes.—This is a symbol of pleasant events, stirring topics and sometimes of personal honour and distinction.

Pudding.—See **Plum Pudding**.

Puffin.—This bird denotes timidity and a desire for solitude; if flying, news from abroad.

Pulpit.—A love of talking and a dislike to listening is the meaning of this symbol.

Pump.—Your own efforts will bring about a fortunate result.

Punch-and-Judy.—You will read, or hear, of a sensational case in married life.

Purse.—This cautions you against theft, or carelessness that may lead to losing money.

Pyramids.—These foreshow attainment to honour, fame and wealth.

Q

Queen.—A queen upon her throne indicates security, peace, and honour; sometimes the attainment to a high position through powerful friends.

Query.—This shows doubt, indecision; if this sign were seen with a letter the doubt would be with regard to some correspondence; if with a journey, uncertainty about it; and so on.

Quill Pen.—This shows that you may expect, before long, to sign your maiden name for the last time in a marriage register; with other signs, a legal document.

Quoits.—This sign indicates a journey to the country on pleasure.

R

Rabbit.—An indication of illness for a child; a dead rabbit means domestic duties which will bore you, sometimes financial worry; several rabbits suggest that you must depend upon your own efforts for your amusements and must be content with simple ones; a rabbit on its hind legs predicts that a new plan or idea will bring you great success.

Rag Doll.—This implies a simplicity that sometimes verges on folly.

Railway Signal.—This symbol may be seen at "danger" or "all clear." Its meaning must be read in accordance with other signs.

Ram.—An unpleasant person whom you would do well to avoid is indicated by this sign.

Rake.—This implement denotes a persevering nature which should bring you a liberal measure of success in whatever you undertake; it also indicates luck in speculation.

Rat.—Treachery and other impending troubles, are foreshown by this unpleasant symbol.

Raven.—This bird is an omen of gloom and despondency, disappointment in love, separation, failure in work; it is also a symbol of death for the aged.

Razor.—Quarrels, also a warning against interference in other people's affairs; to lovers this sign foretells disagreement and separation.

Red-Hot Poker.—This flower suggests that you are likely to bring yourself within the range of unpleasant criticism by your flaunting manner.

Reptile.—This is a bad omen of coming misfortune, treachery, or illness.

Rhinoceros.—This animal denotes a risky proceeding into which you plunge without hesitation, although your friends and relations will try to persuade you to give up your scheme, but your indifference to the opinion of others prevents any chance of their being successful.

Rider.—This brings good news from overseas of business and financial affairs.

Rifle.—Strife and calamity are shown by this sign.

Ring.—With dots around, a contract or a business transaction; with the figures of a man and woman, an engagement or wedding is foretold.

River.—A sign of trouble and perplexity, sometimes illness and bereavement.

Robin.—A symbol of much good fortune, loyal friends, and happiness in love.

Rocket.—This foretells joy and gladness at some event about to happen.

Rocking Chair.—This indicates contemplation of a new idea or scheme about which you are somewhat doubtful.

Rocking Horse.—Happy associations will be renewed; pleasure with children.

Rocks.—These prepare you for alarms and agitation, but if good signs appear, you will eventually find a smooth path through your fife.

Roller.—See **Garden Roller**.

Rolling Pin.—This is an indication that you will be capable of smoothing out your difficulties and will usually find an easy path in which to tread.

Rose.—A token of good fortune, joy, and love.

Rosemary.—Memories of the past will mar your future.

Running Figures.—You may expect an emergency in which you will need to have all your wits about you; sometimes this signifies urgent messages.

S

Sack.—This predicts an unlooked for event which will turn out to be most fortunate.

Saddle.—The successful solving of a troublesome matter is the meaning of this sign.

Sailor.—You may expect news from overseas of an interesting nature.

Salmon Jumping in a Pool.—This is a fortunate sign of propitious news which will mean a great deal to you.

Saucepan.—This is an indication that many troubles will befall you, and your courage will be tested in meeting them.

Sausages.—These show complaints or affliction.

Saw.—Interference which will bring a good deal of trouble upon you, is signified by a saw.

Scaffold.—This signifies that you will enter into a rash speculation.

Scales.—This symbol stands for legal proceedings.

Scarecrow.—This warns you to avoid interfering in the private affairs of others, or you may find that you will receive the cold shoulder from them.

Sceptre.—This is a fortunate sign of distinction and honour.

Scimitar.—You will hear of murders, horrible treachery, and riots.

Scissors.—An unlucky sign of friction between friends; disputing and disagreeableness with married couples; quarrels between lovers; trouble in business.

Scoop.—See **Coal Scoop**.

Screw.—With a little ingenuity and perseverance, you will arrive at that for which you aim.

Screw-Spanner.—Troublesome affairs and vexations are before you.

Scuttle.—See **Coal Scuttle**.

Scythe.—This sign foreshows grief and pain.

Seagull.—A sign of storms; if flying, news from abroad.

Seakale.—A satisfactory conclusion to a vexed question is the meaning of this symbol.

Seal.—An indication that a considerable amount of patience will be necessary before your hopes are realised, but eventually you will gain success and wealth.

Sealing-Wax.—Theoretically you are wise, but you seldom bring your wisdom to bear on practical matters.

See-Saw.—Unless you endeavour to become more decisive and reliable, you will lose any good opportunities which may come your way.

Seaweed.—This denotes a joy in the past of which only the memory remains.

Shamrock.—A sign of good luck.

Shark.—An ominous sign of death.

Shaving-Brush.—This sign suggests that you are apt to turn molehills into mountains.

Sheep.—To landowners or those engaged in any agricultural pursuits sheep are an omen of success and prosperous dealing; to others this sign implies that they will receive assistance from unexpected quarters.

Shell.—Good luck from an unexpected source; with other signs, a visit to the seaside.

Shepherd.—The appearance of this symbol warns you against taking unnecessary risks in all matters.

Ship.—News from distant lands; a successful journey; a voyage.

Shirt.—This sign is considered an omen of good fortune.

Shoes.—These indicate speedy new arrangements which are likely to turn out extremely well.

Shrimping Net.—Pleasures and amusements, unconventionality, and good spirits.

Shutters.—This sign proclaims the fact that there is need for secrecy, and that there may be things in your life of which you trust nothing will be known.

Sickle.—A sign that you will experience sorrow and pain through the callous behaviour of someone you love.

Signpost.—This symbol must be read in conjunction with surrounding symbols; it usually emphasises the importance of other signs; a broken signpost indicates, that you take a wrong turning in your life and afterwards have much cause to regret it.

Skeleton.—This implies a feeling of disgust at some information which is told to you and which you are asked not to reveal.

Skipping Rope.—Pleasure with children and popularity with them.

Sleigh.—A spell of cold weather; an interesting event or piece of news to be expected in the winter.

Slug.—Petty annoyances; bad weather.

Snail.—This is a sign of infidelity; several snails, that mischief is going on around you of which you are unaware.

Snake.—This is an unpleasant sign of treachery, disloyalty, and hidden danger, sometimes caused by those whom you least suspect; if its head is raised, injury by the malice of a man is predicted; it is also an indication of misfortune and illness.

Snipe.—This bird signifies the discovery of a useful fact; if flying, hasty news of a great friend.

Snowdrops.—These are a symbol of youth and innocence; this sign may point to some event affecting you and yours which will probably take place about February; if seen in a cross it would foreshow the death of an infant or young child.

Soap.—Cakes or blocks of soap predict temporary trouble in business.

Soap Bubbles.—See **Child Blowing Soap Bubbles**.

Sofa.—This foreshows indisposition or a small illness, sometimes disturbed nights or emergencies.

Soldier.—This signifies that you may count upon the loyalty and affection of your friends; sometimes it indicates that you may expect speedy news of a soldier.

Solomon's Seal.—This plant is a symbol of understanding, devotion, and coming joy.

Soup Ladle.—It will be through the assistance of others that you will arrive at success.

Soup Tureen.—To the mature, this symbol points to a return of good fortune; to the young, a small illness and loss of appetite.

Spade.—This means toil, care, unrest, disappointment, and failure. See **Ace of Spades**.

Spanner.—See **Screw Spanner**.

Sphinx.—This denotes that your hopes will be set on things far beyond your reach, and that as nothing but the very best in life has any attraction for you, it is improbable that you will ever attain to complete happiness.

Spider.—You may expect to receive an inheritance; with other signs, that you will be triumphant in disputed will or money settlement; several spiders foretell profitable transactions, sometimes a heritage of much wealth.

Spur.—This symbol foretells that as the result of endurance and honest labour you will attain to honour.

Square.—This formed of dotted lines indicates perplexity and dismay, and endeavour to extricate yourself from an embarrassing situation.

Squirrel.—This is a sign of contentment and cheerfulness; although you may never be rich you will be loved by those around you and, on the whole, will lead a happy life.

Star.—A lucky sign; if surrounded by dots, wealth and honour are foretold.

Steamer.—A voyage, news from overseas, interesting events, according to other signs.

Steeple.—This denotes misfortune, bad luck; if it is crooked or bending it foreshows a coming disaster or crushing blow to your hope.

Steps.—Unaccustomed work which will fall to your lot as a result of the illness of someone with whom you work or associate.

Stile.—With a small amount of perception you will arrive at a right conclusion.

Stilts.—These show a desire to appear different in the eyes of your friends from that which you really are, and you will often fail in an effort to keep up this subterfuge.

Stocks.—These sweet scented flowers foreshow an unexpected happiness with someone whom you have not seen for a long while.

Stockings.—A present received or given is the meaning of this symbol.

Stones.—Little worries and vexations.

Stool.—A large stool is a symbol of honour; a small one signifies that your success in life will be meagre.

Stork.—In summer, this bird tells you to beware of robbery or fraud; in winter, prepare for bad weather and a great misfortune; a stork flying predicts that whilst you hesitate in coming to a decision, a profitable chance is lost, the news of which will speedily reach you.

Stove.—This symbol calls attention to the fact that trials and tribulations await you.

Straw.—A bundle of straw foretells gain through industry.

Strawberries.—Pleasure and the gratification of your wishes are shown by this fruit.

Straw Hat.—Modesty and simple pleasures.

Street Lamp.—This is a sign of a foolish desire to draw attention to yourself.

Stud.—See **Collar Stud**.

Stuffed Birds.—A discovery that something upon which you had set your heart proves unsatisfying.

Submarine.—Swiftly arriving news or events; sometimes the disclosure of a secret which will be of much personal value to you.

Sun.—This promises happiness, health, success in love, prosperity, and the beneficial discovery of secrets.

Sun Bonnet.—A sign of originality, personal charm and attraction, sometimes coquetry.

Sundial.—You are warned to take heed as to the way in which you spend your time.

Sunflower.—This flower proclaims learning and a satisfactory conclusion in matters which are most interesting to you; it also implies that you may reasonably expect a scheme to work out greatly to your advantage.

Suspenders.—These show precaution.

Suspension Bridge.—A venture in which much is at stake but after a time of anxiety you arrive at final triumph.

Swallow.—A journey with a happy result; if flying, joyful tidings from someone you love; if several swallows are flying, they indicate a journey to a warm climate under very pleasant conditions.

Swan.—This bird is significant of tribulation, troublesome conditions in the home, and sometimes of separation from those whom you love.

Sweep.—The performing of an urgent disagreeable business will shortly fall to your lot.

Sweet William.—This flower signifies that happiness in the past has tinged your future with sadness.

Swimming.—A brave endeavour to overcome your fear of an undertaking which must be faced.

Swing-Boat.—By an act of folly, you forfeit the good opinion of someone with whom you most desire to be on terms of friendship.

Sword.—This is a sign of danger, sudden illness, or even death; it also betokens slander and dangerous gossip; to lovers it is a bad omen of quarrels; a sword in its sheath shows honour and glory for someone dear to you; a broken sword predicts the triumph of an enemy.

T

Table.—This means suggestions and consultation; note the subject from the surrounding signs.

Tambourine.—A symbol of lighthearted gaiety which will follow a time of gloom or worry. See also **Child with Tambourine**.

Tea Cosy.—To the unmarried, this is a sign that they will probably remain single; to the married, affection and comfort in the small things of life.

Tea-Cup and Saucer.—You may expect to hear something of much interest and pleasure in your "fortune."

Teeth.—These call attention to the fact that probably a visit to the dentist is required.

Telegraph Post.—Hasty news by telephone or telegram.

Telegraph Wires.—You will transact important business by telephone or telegram.

Telephone.—You will be put to considerable inconvenience through forgetfulness.

Telescope.—This predicts the probability of trouble with your eyesight.

Tennis Net.—This shows pleasures and social entertainments.

Tent.—A symbol of travel.

Thimble.—For a girl, this symbol implies that she will probably never marry; to the married, it predicts changes in the household.

Thistle.—This is a pleasant sign of strength, endurance, and affection; it also shows a desire to remove obstacles from the path of those who are in difficulties.

Throne.—An empty throne denotes public misfortune. See also **King on Throne**.

Thumb.—A large and powerful thumb foretells an opportunity in which you prove yourself superior to those who hitherto somewhat despised you.

Tiger.—You will be placed in a perilous position possibly through the bad behaviour or folly of those who should protect you.

Timber.—Logs of timber are a sign of well-being and prosperity in your affairs.

Tin Tacks.—An agreement about to be satisfactorily concluded.

Toad.—You may expect deceit and the discovery of disagreeable facts; this sign should caution you to be on your guard, for malicious talking causes much discomfort and may separate the best of friends.

Toadstool.—You are warned against making rash and unguarded statements, a bad habit of gossiping and encouraging scandal.

Tomatoes Growing.—An increase of worldly goods is foreshown by this sign.

Tombstone.—This sign must be judged in accordance with other symbols around it.

Tongs.—A pair of firetongs indicates anxiety and disturbance in the home.

Tongue.—This signifies that unless you amend you will make mischief by your indiscreet and unkind words.

74

Tooth.—One large tooth is a symbol of bereavement.

Topiary Work.—Trees and hedges cut into the forms of birds, animals, etc., are often to be seen in the tea-leaves; this sign assures you of the fact that those things for which you must wait longest are those which will give most joy.

Torch (Flaming).—This is a hopeful symbol that some unexpected piece of good fortune will come to you; it also indicates the discovery of an undeveloped talent.

Torpedo.—Acts of violence, disaster, or distressing news are the meanings of this symbol.

Tortoise.—This means that you attempt that of which you have no knowledge.

Tower.—This predicts an advantageous opportunity through which you may rise to a good position in life.

Toys.—Pleasure with children.

Train.—Arrivals, removals, a journey.

Tram.—A roadway journey on business or pleasure.

Tram Line.—This is indicated by two thin, straight lines which run near together up the side of the cup.

Trees.—Good health and a pleasing assurance of coming prosperity and happiness; if surrounded by dots an inheritance of property in the country is foreshown! See also **Chestnut Tree, Christmas Tree, Elm Tree, Oak Tree, Yew Tree**.

Triangle.—A fortunate meeting, good luck; sometimes an unexpected legacy.

Trident.—A hopeful sign of honour and promotion to those in the Navy.

Triumphal Arch.—This is a fortunate omen of your future honour and high position; a decorated arch foretells a wedding.

Trowel.—This gardening implement foretells good weather conditions; seen in the winter, it indicates unusual mildness. See also **Bricklayer's Trowel**.

Trousers.—A pair of trousers foretells news of misfortune or sorrow for a man.

True Lover's Knot.—This is a happy omen of faithfulness in love, and of enduring friendship.

Trumpet.—This denotes good fortune to a musician; to others, entertainment, large assemblies of people, public speaking, sometimes the setting on foot of new schemes.

Trunk.—Arrivals and departures.

Tub.—You have evil to fear, is the meaning of this sign.

Tulips.—A symbol of radiance, health, and constancy in love and friendship.

Tunnel.—This suggests that you are likely to make a wrong decision in an important matter.

Turkey.—That you are in danger of committing injurious follies is the meaning of this sign.

Turnip.—The discovery of secrets and domestic quarrels are indicated by this sign.

Turnpike.—This implies that the reminiscences which you relate of the past are of more interest than your topics of the present.

Turnstile.—This is a sign that you cleverly evade a disagreeable incident or unpleasant discussion without offending anyone.

Turtle.—This is significant of wealth and luxury.

Twins.—This is a symbol of sympathy and the perfection of happiness; with other signs, news of the birth of twins.

U

Ugly Faces.—These show domestic quarrels or unpleasant news.

Umbrella.—If it is open, bad weather and grumbling are foretold; closed, a bit of bad luck which may be avoided.

Unicorn.—This is an indication of scandal.

Urn.—A sign of illness.

V

Vampire.—This brings a message of gloom and sorrow, or also means that you await the expected news of a death.

Van.—This sign denotes an interesting experiment in which you succeed.

Vanity Bag.—A large circle of admiring friends, and much pleasure with them.

Vase.—This sign brings you a promise of good health.

Vegetable Marrow.—This means sad news or monetary losses through bad crops, either at home or abroad.

Vegetables.—These indicate toil, followed by a time of leisure and affluent circumstances.

Venus.—This planet which is sometimes seen in the tea-leaves, brings a message of peace or placidity.

Vise.—A carpenter's vise signifies that you will need powerful assistance to extricate you from the mess in which you will find yourself through your folly.

Violets.—This is a symbol of high ideals and of the finding of happiness in its fullest sense; several violets assure you of coming joy; if in the form of a cross, death is predicted.

Violin.—A symbol of coming success to a musician, and of pleasure and entertainment to others.

Vulture.—This bird is a forewarning of evil and unrest in various quarters of the globe; it also means a powerful enemy, sometimes death; if it flies, tragedy, sorrow, and tears are predicted.

W

Wading Boot.—This is a warning to be cautious in swimming or boating, or you may meet with an accident; with other signs it denotes a home by the sea.

Wagon.—This implies a fortunate outlook and changes for the better.

Walking Stick.—The arrival of a male visitor.

Wall.—A thick, high wall denotes many difficulties in your life, and that much courage will be needed to overcome them.

Wallflower.—This sign indicates the serious consideration of a new plan.

Warming Pan.—This is a sign of comfort in small things and domestic peace.

Wasps.—These insects are significant of distress caused by the sharp tongues of those around you.

Water.—This is usually recognised by a clear space entirely free from tea-leaves at the bottom of the cup.

Water Lily.—This flower proclaims a declaration of love.

Weasel.—This animal shows cunning, and points to the sly behaviour of someone with whom you associate, and of whom you feel no suspicion.

Weathercock.—This is a sign that you feel incapable of making up your mind definitely on any matter without first consulting each one with whom you come in contact, and in the end you settle upon an entirely different course of action.

Wedding Cake.—This proclaims a speedy and prosperous marriage.

Whale.—A prediction of personal danger which may be averted if you are cautious.

Wheel.—This is symbolic of the wheel of fortune and foreshows a prosperous career or an inheritance of wealth; a broken wheel predicts a bad disappointment as to an expected increase of income or a legacy.

Wheelbarrow.—This sign foretells a visit to the country or a pleasant renewal of friendship with those who live in it.

Whip.—To a woman this sign foretells vexation and trials in her marriage; for a man, it has much the same meaning, and severe disappointment will befall him.

Wicket Gate.—A small incident leads up to an important future event.

Widow's Bonnet.—This sign must be read in connection with other symbols; sometimes it foreshows grief and mourning, or if dots are round it, that a sum of money or a legacy may be expected from a widow.

Windmill.—A sign that you may hope to succeed in a doubtful enterprise.

Window.—An open window shows that you are regarded with favour by many; a closed one means embarrassment.

Wine Cup.—Joy and realised ambition.

Witch on Broom.—You will be reproved by some of your friends who consider that your interest in psychic matters is dangerous, but later on you will be able to prove to their satisfaction that no harm has come to it.

Witness Box.—With bad signs around it, this would point to a personal matter ending in a law court; otherwise, it denotes the taking place of a trial in which you will feel special interest.

Wolf.—Beware of an avaricious and hard-hearted neighbour or friend.

Woman Carrying a Burden.—An unhappy marriage or unfortunate love affair.

Woman Carrying a Child.—This shows distress, sometimes illness of someone dear to you, or sadness through separation.

Woman Holding a Mirror.—Clairvoyance and prediction of the future are signified by this symbol.

Women.—With bad signs, several women mean scandal; otherwise, society.

Wood.—Much happiness with someone dear to you, a forthcoming wedding, or a fortunate and favourable event.

Woodpecker.—This bird brings pleasant news from those who live in the country.

Worms.—These warn you of coming misfortune, or of treachery, and evil by secret foes.

Wreath.—This is a symbol of marriage, and of much happiness being in store for you.

Y

Yacht.—This is a favourable sign of increased wealth or happiness.

Yew Tree.—You may expect to attain to a prominent position in life, and to receive a legacy from an aged relative or friend.

Z

Zebra.—Something for which you have long waited is now within sight, but you are likely to be disappointed, for you will find that it was not worth waiting for after all.

Some Combinations of Symbols

And Their Meaning

Ace of Diamonds, A Circle.—An engagement.

Ace of Diamonds, A Bush.—A pleasant invitation.

Ace of Clubs, An Obelisk.—The offer of a good promotion.

Ace of Hearts, A Train, A Query.—Indecision about a removal.

Ace of Hearts, An Urn, A Bed.—Illness in the home.

Ace of Spades, Bricks.—An advantageous offer from a large town.

Arm, A Myrtle Tree, Bird on a Perch.—New plans which bring about a meeting with someone who will become all the world to you.

Arum Lily, Bells, A Church.—A wedding.

Arum Lily, A Bat, A Bed, A Widow's Bonnet.—Death of a widow.

Bacon, Pagoda.—You will make your fortune abroad.

Banana, A Peacock, Ace of Hearts, Trees.—A happy marriage to someone of wealth and property in the country.

Bed, An Engine, Laburnum Tree.—A happy visit to the country in the spring.

Besom, Ugly Faces.—You will make many enemies by mischief-making.

Bonnet, A Bouquet.—Marriage late in life.

Bride, A Crescent Moon, A Swallow.—A journey which leads to a romantic love affair.

Bride, Penknife, An Owl.—Jealousy terminates an unhappy engagement.

Cab, A Square, A Cap.—A gloomy outlook brought about by one of the opposite sex.

Camel (Laden), A Small "T", A Coffin.—An unexpected fortune through the death of someone abroad whose name begins with "T".

Chain (Entangled), Onion.—You will be placed in an embarrassing position by the discovery of a secret.

Clover, Plums, A Bridge.—A new and excellent opportunity will come your way necessitating a journey.

Daffodils, The Sun.—A joyful occurrence in the spring.

Doves, A Book, A Beehive.—You will advance rapidly and become a well-known writer.

Duck, A Vegetable Marrow.—Rash investments.

Eagle (Flying), A Steamer, A Tent, A Large "E".—A position of honour in Egypt.

Ear, A Beehive, A Trumpet.—Fame as a public speaker.

Fate Line, A Sword in Its Sheath, The Sign of Mars, A Chain.—A happy fate awaits you, and marriage to a soldier who will rise to the top of the tree in his profession.

Frog, A Fish, A Ship, A Large "C".—Emigration to Canada.

Goat, A Running Figure, A Lamb.—There need be no doubt as to the successful outcome of your venture.

Grasshoppers, A Sleigh, A Wreath of Asters.—Death of an elderly friend or relative in the winter.

Key, A Flaming Torch.—Some discovery or the development of a patent leads to your becoming famous.

King on His Throne, An Eagle in a Cage, A Mace.— An important public ceremony in which you take a part.

Ladder, Ring, A Man and a Woman.—Marriage will be the means of advancement and good fortune.

Ladder, A Palette.—Attainment to a position of honour as an artist.

Ladder, The Symbol of Mars.—A most fortunate career as a soldier.

Lion, A Lute.—Rising to the top of the tree, as a musician, is assured by these symbols.

Lion, A Man Speaking from a Platform.—Great success in a public career and the attaining to an influential position.

Lion, A Man Beside a Pestle and Mortar.—Excellent prospects and fame as a doctor.

Lizard, A Peaked Cap.—An expected visitor is not to be trusted.

Mace, A Mallet.—Through wisdom and clear judgment you will rise to a position of authority.

Man Carrying a Burden, A Pair of Scissors, A Mushroom.—Quarrels in an unhappy love affair ending in a broken engagement.

Magnet, A Meat Cover.—An unpleasant discovery leads to the abrupt ending of an infatuation.

Nail, A Pair of Pincers.—A visit to the dentist and the removal of a tooth.

Notice-Board, A Leek, An Open Padlock.—In a surprising manner you will get the information for which you are seeking.

Onions, An Otter.—Those in whom you trusted have betrayed your confidence and divulged a secret.

Owl, A Pail.—Loss of income will necessitate your undertaking distasteful work.

Pagoda, A Palm Tree, Water.—A voyage to a warm climate under very happy conditions.

Pestle and Mortar, A Walking Stick.—Illness and the arrival of the doctor.

Pulpit, Opera Glasses.—Those who weary others by undue curiosity will always remain in ignorance.

Query, A Letter, Initial "B", A Grave Stone.—You will be consulted as to the erecting of a headstone on the grave of a relative or friend.

Quill Pen, Lilies of the Valley, An Organ.—Great happiness through marriage.

Rabbit, An Arrow, A Large Letter "L", A Dagger.—News of severe illness and a probable operation for a child who lives in London.

Rhinoceros, An Overcoat, A Steamer, A Large Letter "I".—The undertaking of a somewhat hazardous enterprise necessitates a voyage to India; through this much will happen which will eventually lead to your becoming famous.

Rocket, A Pear, A Snowdrop.—News of a birth of which you may expect to hear in February.

Rocking Chair, A Pedestrian, A Mushroom.— Deliberation over important matters brings you to the conclusion that a great venture, which may mean enormous gain, is worth a small risk, and success will await you.

Sailor, A Flying Swallow, A Trident, A Ring.—Happy news of good promotion for a sailor and a proposal of marriage.

Scaffold, Leg of Mutton.—Gambling or speculation will bring you to poverty unless you pay heed to this warning.

Shark, A Pistol, A Flying Seagull.—News from abroad of a tragic death.

Snake, A Ram, A Woman, A Widow's Bonnet.—Overwhelming evidence against some widow who is a dangerous enemy.

Sofa, A Sleigh.—A cold in the head or a chill.

Sword, A Ring, A Man, A Woman, A Toad.—Separation of lovers brought about by slander and malicious talk.

Table, A Quill Pen, A Cat, A Ring with Dots Around.—Legal business over money matters which leads to family quarrels.

Throne, An Ostrich Running, A Flying Seagull, A Flag.—Serious news from abroad of disturbances and rebellion.

Tram Lines, A Building with Dots Around It, A Purse.—You will take a roadway journey to a bank and are warned to beware of pickpockets.

Urn, Hospital Nurse, A Man, A Large Heart.—Serious illness affecting the heart is predicted for a man.

Violet, A Water Lily, A Robin, A Crescent Moon, A Ring.—A romantic love affair which ends in a happy marriage taking place in the early spring.

Wading Boot, The Sign of Neptune, Several Penguins, A Mast.— News of a disaster in the North Sea.

Widow's Bonnet, A Pig, A Dotted Circle, The Figures "100".—A small legacy of a hundred pounds may be expected from a widow.

Woodpecker, Trees, A Rose, A Man.—A prospective visit to the country in the summer, when you will meet with someone who will become very dear to you.

Yew Tree, An Open Padlock, A Wallflower, A Pineapple.—A new plan of life is made necessary as the result of an unexpected inheritance of much wealth.

Some Example Cups
with Their Interpretations

The following twenty illustrations are photographs of cups which on various occasions have been turned by consultants and interpreted by a seer. The student will find these of much practical value in learning what symbols to look for, and how to discern them clearly as the cup is turned about in the hand.

The divination of each cup should be carefully studied with its illustration; by this means the student will be enabled to grasp the principles upon which to form a judgment of the cup as a whole.

Having mastered this, the knowledge gained can be supplemented by reference to the alphabetical Dictionary of Symbols and Their Meanings in the previous chapter.

To study the illustrations and their descriptions correctly, the former must be turned about and about until each symbol has been identified.

Twenty Illustrations
with Their Interpretations

INTERPRETATION FIGURE I

The most noticeable feature of this cup is the clear evidence given that the chief interests of the consultant are bound up in some man in India. That there is delay in receiving important news from him is shown by the symbol of the pigeon on the stone immediately beneath the handle. But that most favourable news may be expected later is certain, for the figure of a man upon an elephant with a pineapple beyond gives proof of this. The child's toys show the consultant's association and happiness with children. The figure of the woman seated on the edge of a rock with its curious peak behind her, and the seagull below, suggest that storms at sea will cause distress to some woman known to the consultant. The small figure "11," close to this symbol, points out that it is likely to be eleven days before there is hope of the anxiety being relieved.

FIGURE I

PRINCIPAL SYMBOLS

On sides.—Large letter "P." Child's toys. Woman with uplifted hands on curious shaped rock. Small numeral "11" above. Seagull perched on small rock beneath.

In centre.—Pigeon standing on large stone, man in sun helmet on elephant. Sign-post pointing to letter "P."

Near rim and handle.—A pineapple on dish.

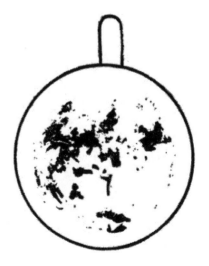

INTERPRETATION FIGURE II

This cup shows that a variety of events may be expected, with a fair proportion of pleasure and success to be anticipated from them.

The finger beyond the handle pointing to the ark indicates that in all trials the consultant will find a refuge. The hanging lamp is also a guarantee of coming success, and prosperous undertakings, in some new plan which is under consideration.

The clouds, the symbol of the goat beyond which is facing into the open gateway, signify that an advantageous opportunity, to which a certain amount of risk is attached, awaits the consultant; the prominent figurehead upon the stone pillar gives assurance that all will turn out well, and that there is no need for hesitation in embarking upon this new opportunity; that it will necessitate a removal is shown by the buildings beyond. The quill pen and dots point to the fact that some legal business will be transacted over money affairs.

The dove-cot in the centre, with the form of a widow with dots around, signifies that a benefit to the home may be expected in the future, through a widow. The clergyman in conjunction, holding a paper, shows that the benefit will probably come about through a reconciliation. The bank of clouds behind the ferry boat shows that some trouble, to be expected in the future, will be lightened by the help of good friends. Whilst the bird stationary upon the piece of wood, at some distance from the consultant, and in conjunction with the letter "L," means uncertainty as to some desired information, which should come from someone whose name begins with "L."

FIGURE II

PRINCIPAL SYMBOLS

On sides.—Finger. Small ark. Hanging lamp and shade. Large armchair. Bank of clouds. Goat. Large open gateway. Curious shaped figurehead upon a stone pillar. Low curved wall and buildings. Small quill pen and dots.

In centre.—Dove-cot. Widow in flowing veil seated in chair. Dots around. Man in clerical hat holding an open paper in his hand.

Near rim.—Shapeless leaves. Small ferry boat on water. Bird standing on log of wood. Letter "L".

INTERPRETATION FIGURE III

The cat with dots around being near the handle indicates financial worry in the home. The bone beyond shows that the misfortunes will be met with courage, and eventually overcome. The cockatoo, with the cauliflower appearing on the opposite side, signifies that an unreliable friend will cause the consultant a little uneasiness, and as a small symbol of a mushroom is beside it, a quarrel with this undesirable friend may be expected.

The pear may be linked to the symbol of the font in the centre of the cup, showing that the consultant may expect news of a birth; the carving indicates that the news will give much satisfaction; the wine-cup, with the leg in conjunction, points out that the ambitions of the consultant will certainly be realised in the future. That a certain amount of waiting will be necessary is shown by the distance from the handle.

The motor boat, and monument in the centre, foretell the successful outcome of a new venture, which at present is unthought-of. The rocks show that a certain amount of mental agitation is aroused by the setting out on this undertaking, but, with the reassuring symbols in this cup, no alarm is necessary.

FIGURE III

PRINCIPAL SYMBOLS

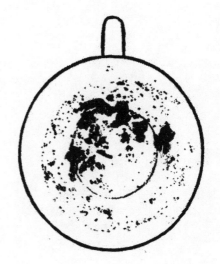

On side under handle.—Cat. Scattered dots.

On side.—Bone. Cockatoo upon a stump of wood. Small symbol of a leg. Wine-cup held in hand. Small symbol of a mushroom. Pear. Cauliflower.

On circle under handle.—Curious shaped rocks.

On circle beyond.—Monument.

In centre.—Motor boat. Font. Carved figures.

INTERPRETATION FIGURE IV

The symbol of the seal being directly under the handle, with the large arch and carving beyond, show that the consultant will soon enjoy the fulfilment of a long desired hope; everything is going smoothly, and will turn out as desired. The only obstacle is seen in the symbol of the weasel, which appears beyond the seal, pointing to the fact that the consultant has someone who is not to be trusted in the home, but this will not result in anything serious.

The figures of the two women opposite the handle show the arrival of friends to the "house," bringing presents with them. The inkpot, pen, and numeral "7," with the bird's nest in connection, show that happy news, as the result of personal effort on the part of the consultant, may be looked for within seven days.

The rock, motor, and wavy lines being in conjunction, warn the consultant of some forthcoming vexation, and possibly alarm, in connection with a motor expedition, but the episode is in the distance, and will not be more than a passing cloud.

The slug, at the bottom of the cup, predicts a future disturbance with someone, but the matter will be trifling. The large symbol of the king and queen upon the throne, opposite the handle, foretells a future of honour and wealth, and the assurance of every happiness for this fortunate consultant.

FIGURE IV

PRINCIPAL SYMBOLS

Opposite handle on circle.—Two women, inside figure carrying basket, outside figure with parcel under arm.

On sides.—Line of wavy dots. Large rock. Motor. Bird's nest. Pen. Numeral "7." Inkpot.

On circle.—Large arch with carving.

In centre.—Slug. Figures of King

and Queen on throne.

Under handle.—Seal. Weasel.

INTERPRETATION FIGURE V

The large rock on the side, with the letter "J" beside it, speaks of a forthcoming vexation or trouble caused by someone whose name begins with "J." The necklace and jewellery beyond, with scattered dots around, give a cheerful assurance to the consultant of coming prosperity. This is further emphasised by the circle of dots above the letter "C" in the centre. As the initial is large, it probably indicates the name of the place from which the source of wealth may be anticipated; and that much happiness will come to the consultant in the future, is shown by the dancing figure and carved figures being in conjunction.

The small basket, the sausage, and roll of bread, with the query and "2" beyond, all point to the fact that the consultant will have little complaints and grumbles to put up with, and there will be some doubt as to which of two people is most to blame. But it will be only a small ripple upon the otherwise smooth surface of the consultant's outlook.

FIGURE V

PRINCIPAL SYMBOLS

On sides.—Large rocks. Letter "J" in conjunction. Necklace. Jewelry.

In centre.—Large ornamental "C." Circle of dots above. Figure of girl dancing with arm upraised beneath. Carved figures.

In centre near circle.—Basket. Large sausage with roll of bread in conjunction. Small query. Numeral "2."

INTERPRETATION FIGURE VI

The numeral "4," beside the shapeless leaves, and the line leading from this to the flat rock beyond, indicate that in about four days the consultant may expect to meet with obstacles in the way of some prospective outing or pleasure, which will probably fall through.

The corkscrew, with the letter "C" in conjunction, signifies vexatious curiosity as to the consultant's private concerns, on the part of persons whose names begin with these initials. But that it is merely a passing annoyance is shown by the symbol of the arch, and dancing figures above it, and, with the fig tree beyond, foretells the development of things most wished for, and much future happiness and prosperity.

The anvil in the centre, with the branches of a tree in conjunction, suggests that it will be largely owing to the consultant's energy that this hopeful outlook in the future may safely be predicted.

FIGURE VI

PRINCIPAL SYMBOLS

On sides.—Corkscrew. Letter "C." Arch. Dancing figures above. Fig tree.

Near rim.—Shapeless leaves. Numeral "4." Line leading to flat rock.

In centre.—Anvil. Branches of a tree.

Under handle.—Scattered dots.

INTERPRETATION FIGURE VII

Although the small symbol of the dagger points towards the consultant, it would not in this case predict a personal danger, as there are no further signs of illness or misfortune. So that it may safely be taken to mean that the consultant will shortly be going to see a friend who has had an operation; this fact is borne out by the short dotted line beyond, leading to the door knocker, under which is written the word "in."

The numeral "7" coming at the end of the dotted line would show that it will probably be seven weeks before this friend recovers from the illness. This friend's name is shown to begin with "L," as that letter is also near the end of the lines.

The more distant signs of a brooch and a cabinet beyond both foretell the unexpected development of good fortune. If the consultant is married, the thimble in the centre would show future changes in the household; that they will be advantageous is shown by the large feather which gives assurance of a prosperous future.

That this may come about through a friend, or lover, is shown by the cigar, and is further emphasised by the large dots beside it.

A warning against extravagance, however, is given to the consultant by the crinoline, which appears amidst these signs of future wealth.

FIGURE VII

PRINCIPAL SYMBOLS

Near rim.—Small dagger. Short dotted line leading to door knocker, with "in" written beneath. Numeral "7". Letter "L". Dots.

On sides near circle.—Group of dots and small symbols showing presents. Brooch. Cabinet.

In centre.—Crinoline. Large feather. Small cigar. Thimble.

Under handle.—Symbols of letters and parcels.

INTERPRETATION FIGURE VIII

The only definite indication of future prospects is shown by the symbol of the organ, and acorn, upon the circle at the bottom of the cup, the position of these signs showing that hope will not be realised for some time.

But these symbols make the prediction of ultimate success a safe one. Should the consultant be a musician, triumph in the profession would be assured.

The coal scoop and beetle are significant of domestic worries and household cares. But the tea cosy in the centre promises compensation in the way of small comforts and affection.

FIGURE VIII

PRINCIPAL SYMBOLS

Small symbol of a coal scoop.

On circle.—Organ. Acorn beside it. Beetle.

In centre.—Tea cosy.

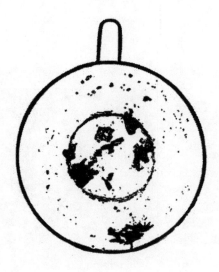

INTERPRETATION FIGURE IX

This cup would be singularly disappointing from the consultant's point of view, as it is devoid of incident.

The large spray of thistle on the rim indicates an unselfish life of endurance. For the present, there is no sign of a more eventful existence.

The dust-pan, brush, and duster, in the centre, point to future domestic vexations, but the large spray of iris beside it promises a pleasure which will far outbalance the trifling disturbance.

FIGURE IX

PRINCIPAL SYMBOLS

Near rim.—Thistle.

Centre.—Dust-pan and brush. Duster. Large spray of iris.

Under handle.—Shapeless leaves.

INTERPRETATION FIGURE X

The most striking features of this cup are the various indications of pleasure and social enjoyment. These being shown by the cake and butterfly, while the orchid in conjunction predicts that the consultant's personal charm and power of attraction will result in a future of wealth and social distinction.

The pillar, near the rim and handle, gives a pleasing assurance of security and loyal friends. The bird flying from the cage brings joyful news, that something which has been an obstacle in the way of the consultant's desires is about to be removed, and much future happiness may be looked for.

The figure of the man fishing from a rock foreshows the arrival of a visitor, who will have some pleasant news to tell.

The toque opposite the handle, but at the bottom of the cup, gives further evidence of the good luck coming to this fortunate consultant.

FIGURE X

PRINCIPAL SYMBOLS

Near rim.—Small stone pillar. Cake on dish. Man on rock fishing.

On sides.—Bird cage, small bird flying from it.

On circle.—Butterfly. Lady's hat.

In centre.—Orchid with long stalk.

Under handle.—Shapeless leaves.

INTERPRETATION FIGURE XI

This cup indicates that the consultant is apt to be ruffled by trifles and to become upset by anything unexpected. As, for instance, in the case of the arrival of visitors, shown by the mass of leaves and chair. The query beside it shows the indecision of the consultant's mind as to necessary arrangements. The boots on the opposite side denote that lack of income will not trouble the consultant.

But that there is some misfortune or hindrance in the future is shown by the symbol of the broken cross in the bottom of the cup; the head and shoulders of the woman beside it suggest that this trouble will be caused by a woman. Compensation will be found in the happy love affair, which is clearly predicted by the cherries, the figures of the man and woman embracing, and the man's hat and pipe.

Large dots signify that wealth will be added to happiness. This event must not be expected for some months, as the symbols are in the bottom of the cup.

The letter "N" with the dots and small tree beyond show an immediate pleasant happening, in connection with a person whose name begins with that letter.

FIGURE XI

PRINCIPAL SYMBOLS

Near rim.—Mass of leaves. Stones.

On sides.—Chair. Query. Two boots.

On circle.—Figure of man and woman embracing. Small bunch of cherries beneath. Several dots. Man's hat and pipe in conjunction.

In centre.—Broken cross. Head and shoulders of woman.

Under handle.—Letter "N." Small tree beyond.

INTERPRETATION FIGURE XII

The present conditions of this consultant are not cheering. The large cloud, associated with dots, the small dog on the opposite side, and the policeman beyond, all point to grievous money worries, possibly caused by dishonesty.

The somewhat indistinct axe implies a brave effort to overcome, and final mastery of, some of the difficulties.

However, the future has more pleasant prospects, and may be looked forward to with hope. The symbols of the clover and cherries, give assurance of this.

The spray of ivy speaks of the patience with which the present trials are borne, also that true friends are a source of comfort to the consultant.

FIGURE XII

PRINCIPAL SYMBOLS

On side.—Small dog lying down.

Near rim.—Policeman. Indistinct symbol of an axe. Large cloud. Dots.

Centre.—Two small butterflies. Small symbol of a stocking. Small bunch of cherries. Spray of ivy. Clover.

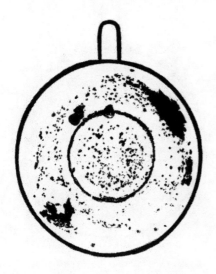

INTERPRETATION FIGURE XIII

The consultant who has "turned" this cup must be prepared for delays, and must not expect real happiness until rather late in life, this being shown by the bonnet and strings on the side of the cup.

The small symbol of birds on a perch gives further evidence that having to wait is a feature of the consultant's lot. The rock and pipe beyond show some dismay with regard to a dear friend.

The large spray of mistletoe and holly at the bottom of the cup, with the letters "F" and "L" in conjunction, implies that some event of importance to the consultant, in connection with persons whose names begin with these initial letters, will occur in the winter. If the cup has been "turned" during the autumn or winter, probably a year will pass before the event takes place, as the mistletoe indicates delay. But this consultant is prepared to hear the truth, and faces it calmly, even if it is a little unpleasant; the symbol of the woman looking into the glass brings this fact to light.

The child playing with its toys foreshows future pleasant plans which will result in tranquillity and satisfaction.

FIGURE XIII

PRINCIPAL SYMBOLS

On sides.—Bonnet and strings. Birds on perch. Pieces of rock. A pipe.

On circle.—Child with toys.

Centre.—Large sprays of mistletoe and holly. Letters "F" and "L." Figure of woman looking in glass.

INTERPRETATION FIGURE XIV

This cup was "turned" by a well-known authoress. Its sinister appearance is accounted for by the fact that at the time of "turning" the cup, she was arranging mentally a murder plot for the book she was then writing.

The symbols speak for themselves and need no explanation.

It is a most interesting specimen, as being absolutely unique.

FIGURE XIV

PRINCIPAL SYMBOLS

On side overlapping circle.—Tail and hindquarters of rat, with head in a hole. Monster with a man's head and bear's paws.

On side.—Dead fish beyond.

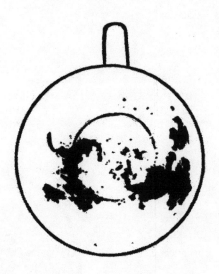

INTERPRETATION FIGURE XV

The consultant who "turned" this cup was sorrowful and had either just passed through a bereavement, or such will take place in the immediate future. The rough cross and the grave near the handle point to this. The bed, with the figure of the woman in nurse's cloak near it tells of serious illness in the home. But this is a future trouble, as the symbols appear at some distance from the handle. The saucepan also bears witness to the general gloom.

The ivy leaves beyond the rough cross show the patience with which the consultant bears the trials; also that good and loyal friends will be a source of comfort.

The small bit of wood and the closed book are symbols of hope, and assure this sad consultant that the expected improvement in affairs will certainly take place and will relieve some of the present anxieties.

This is the most that can be foretold of the future, for there are no signs of pleasant events or definite changes. Indeed, the symbol of the loaf of bread in the centre of the cup shows that monotony and ordinary routine are all that can be predicted from the divination.

FIGURE XV

PRINCIPAL SYMBOLS

Near rim.—Rough cross. Ivy leaves beyond. Large closed book.

On sides.—Log of wood. Bed. Figure of a woman in nurse's cloak beside it. Grave, with small cross.

In centre.—Loaf of bread. Small symbol of a saucepan.

INTERPRETATION FIGURE XVI

This cup gives an impression of a somewhat undeveloped character which is further brought into notice by the stump of a tree on the circle; the hen on a nest, near the handle, points to a home life of comfort and affection.

The egg in the cup, and the duck, show that a risk of threatened disaster, as a result of rash speculation will be averted, and with the symbol of the three boots, fortunate prospects, and the guarantee of hope fulfilled, may safely be predicted for the future.

FIGURE XVI

PRINCIPAL SYMBOLS

On sides.—Hen on nest. Shapeless leaves. Egg in cup.

Near circle opposite handle.—A duck.

On circle.—Stump of tree. Three boots.

INTERPRETATION FIGURE XVII

The figure of the child, with its toys beyond, implies that new plans, to be made very soon, will be most beneficial, and will bring much pleasure to the consultant. But as the sausages and snail are not far distant, there is likely to be a marring of the pleasant conditions, caused by an act of unfaithfulness on the part of someone with whom the consultant is closely connected.

The bellows beyond suggest that the matter is treated with as much philosophy as possible, and with a resolve to make the best of a bad business; the ham also, being in conjunction, it is evident that the episode will not interfere with the consultant's success in life.

The sign post, with the running figure beside it and the large letter "M" beyond, prepare the consultant for startling news, the result of which will be of great importance. The news will come from a place beginning with the letter "M." There is no doubt that the matter will turn out admirably and bring about many advantages, as shown by the spreading branches of the tree; while the grapes beneath promise abundant success and joy.

The large boot-tree and latch-key on the circle beneath the handle predict a fortunate and unexpected gain in the near future. This consultant may look forward with confidence to the pleasures which fate has in store.

FIGURE XVII

PRINCIPAL SYMBOLS

On sides.—Child seated. Toys beyond. Sausages. Snail. Ham. Bellows.

In centre.—Sign post. Running figure beside it. Large letter "M" in conjunction.

On circle.—Tree with spreading branches. Bunch of grapes beneath. Large boot-tree. Latch-key.

INTERPRETATION FIGURE XVIII

The shadow beneath the haycock shows that the consultant will soon be placed in a somewhat trying position and will have considerable difficulty in finding a way out of it.

The future is full of promise and there can be little doubt that the consultant will enjoy the pleasures of prosperity.

A journey to a cold climate to be taken later will result in very propitious news as shown by the symbol of the pheasant.

FIGURE XVIII

PRINCIPAL SYMBOLS

On sides.—Shapeless leaves. Haycock. Shadow beneath.

In centre.—Pair of boots. Spreading branches of a tree. Pheasant flying.

Near circle.—Head of a polar bear.

INTERPRETATION FIGURE XIX

The doll on the side, with the small symbol of a toadstool beside it, gives a warning to the consultant against folly and a bad habit of gossiping when feeling bored in society. The stuffed head of the deer, in this case, shows that much distress is caused by the unguarded talk, and the consultant certainly cannot be described as an "innocent cause."

The various scattered shapeless leaves point to confusion, and a somewhat "happy-go-lucky" nature. The spray of poppies on the circle beneath the handle foreshows that a pleasant experience may be expected in the summer.

The broken gate, with the cross above it, denotes that a new opportunity which awaits the consultant at a future date, will coincide with a time of perplexity and trouble, which fact is further borne out by the running figure below. This being in conjunction with a large letter "Y," implies that the disturbance will arise in connection with a place, the name of which begins with "Y."

FIGURE XIX

PRINCIPAL SYMBOLS

On sides.—Small symbol of a toadstool. Doll. Head of a stuffed deer.

Near rim.—Many shapeless leaves.

On circle.—Spray of poppies.

In centre.—Broken gate with cross above it. Large "Y." Running figure.

INTERPRETATION FIGURE XX

This cup shows confusion and that the consultant was in a state of mental turmoil at the time of "turning" it. But in spite of this drawback there are some interesting facts to be found.

The dotted circles and large ornamental arch point to a most hopeful outlook and to the successful development of some desire at present unattainable.

The various initials and small numerals scattered about show correspondence as to plans and fixing of dates. The bush apple tree speaks of some pleasure which may be looked forward to in the summer.

The dancing figures predict much future happiness; the numerous changes which are likely to come about will all tend to success and the gratifying of the consultant's wishes. And what more cheerful outlook than this can be desired?

FIGURE XX

PRINCIPAL SYMBOLS

On sides.—Scattered shapeless leaves. Several initials. Small numerals. Dotted circles. A large ornamental arch.

Near circle.—Bush apple tree.

In centre.—Dancing and grotesque figures.

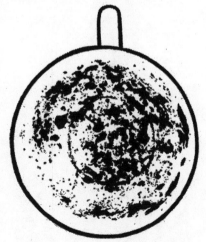

Concluding Note

It may be safely promised to those who follow the simple instructions given in this book that within a short time they will find themselves encircled by a halo of popularity. For few things provide a more certain guarantee of this pleasant condition than that of being able to "tell fortunes". Divination by tea-leaves will bring to those who study it deeply a fund of knowledge beyond the radius of normal understanding.

For those who use it as a means of amusement only, it will give pleasure which is dependent upon nothing more difficult to obtain than a cup of tea! With this recommendation I will leave these pages, in the sincere hope that this little book may be of real value to those who desire to be initiated into the fascinating art of reading the future in a tea-cup.

Made in the USA
Columbia, SC
09 November 2023

25824356R00069